WHOLE

by Natural Harry

WHOLE

by Natural Harry

Down-to-earth plant-based
wholefood recipes

Harriet Birrell

Photographed by Nikole Ramsay

Hardie Grant

BOOKS

Contents

Introduction

The idea for this book came to me as I was enjoying
a delicious hot breakfast while camping on the
shores of Fortescue Bay, enclosed by a wild Tasmanian
coastline. Much of our four-week adventure had forced
us to get back to basics with our food. Frase and
I had a small stove, a knife and a chopping board.
We cooked delicious simple meals in incredible places,
surrounded by nature, in between hiking, surfing and
mountain-bike riding. In getting back to basics in
the Tassie wilderness I unknowingly created a new book.

This book is a careful selection of the recipes that
I made on that trip, but also the recipes I make at
home all the time. You won't find anything elaborate,
challenging or gourmet. This is down-to-earth, good,
whole, satisfying food with a modern twist. It's about
celebrating and enjoying the abundance of wholefoods
available to us and preparing them in a way that is
easy, satisfying and, most importantly, tasty.

For example, refined vegetable oils are replaced with whole fats, such as avocado and coconut. Refined white sugar is replaced with whole vitamin- and mineral-rich versions, such as medjool dates, bananas and maple syrup. Refined flours are replaced with minimally processed whole grains. Only a few recipes contain gluten and for these a gluten-free alternative is suggested in the notes.

My first book, *Natural Harry*, was a collection of summer recipes from our little food caravan. For three summers we provided nourishing treats and smoothies from the wooden caravan that Frase and I built from scratch. During that time, people often asked for my recipes and so the book was all about sharing my secrets from years of refining simple, vibrant plant-based smoothie and raw dessert recipes. We knew that our little caravan was not going to be there forever, so the first book was my way of ensuring that the Natural Harry caravan would live on.

And it has! I have been overwhelmed by the incredible Natural Harry community that has evolved and have loved watching the recipes being recreated and enjoyed again and again.

I have always been interested in the relationship between food and wellbeing. Although my approach has evolved over time, my passion for wholefoods and simplicity has only grown stronger. My food philosophy is quite simple:

'Eat food as close to its natural state as possible and look after yourself. But don't be a goose about it!'

Within these pages you will find more easy weeknight meals like lasagne, meatballs, nachos and pesto pasta. I have also included my favourite hearty salads, go-to nourish bowls, share options and delicious simple brekkies. And it wouldn't be a Natural Harry book if there were no desserts!

So many of life's memorable moments and connections happen over food. With help from Nikole's superb photos, I created this book with family, friends and the wider Natural Harry community in mind. I hope your copy finds a permanent home on the kitchen bench, and becomes lovingly bookmarked and tattered, with the occasional splatter from time spent preparing delicious meals. I hope its pages are filled with the kinds of foods that you want to eat ninety per cent of the time: real, whole, satisfying, nourishing, healthy dishes. True comfort foods.

Harry
x

Tips

Ingredients

The ingredients for these recipes are readily available at grocers, wholefood stores, supermarkets, farmers' markets and your own veggie patch. There are a handful of ingredients I keep on hand that I think make all the difference in plant-based cooking. You can see more information about them, including where to find them, in the Plant-based pantry section on page 281. They are also marked with * in the recipes.

Equipment

There are a few pieces of equipment I find very useful to achieve the best results from these recipes. I recommend a mandoline and a spiraliser. They are both relatively inexpensive and can be very helpful in thinly slicing vegetables or turning them into perfect noodles to spruce up many dishes.

A decent food processor will also make your life easier when it comes to preparing lots of the meals in this book. I recommend investing in a good-quality, high-speed blender. I am asked all too often how to achieve the smoothest sauce, nut cheese, brekkie smoothie and creamiest raw cheesecake or slice. The truth is, it is all in the quality and power of your blender.

Great-quality, chemical-free, non-stick frying pans are also a smart investment to help you avoid having to use refined oils. It is a bonus that they make for much easier cleaning too.

Buy in bulk

Bulk wholefood stores are becoming more and more common these days. They are the perfect place to stock up on your pantry essentials. Take your empty jars and containers and fill them with all the dry staples you need, saving on all the plastic that comes with packaged food. It's better for the environment, your health and your bank balance.

—

Prepare

I am not suggesting hours of food prep here. Simply making a big batch of Miso hummus (see page 266) at the beginning of the week or a jar of Cashew 'parmesan' (see page 272) will go a long way to adding flavour to your meals and saving on time. I also like to stock up on fresh fruit when it is in season, especially bananas. I then peel and freeze them, ensuring that I always have fruit on hand for a delicious smoothie.

Stay well stocked

I like to keep the pantry stocked with all the staples that store well. That way, you'll always have most of the pieces of the recipe puzzle on hand. Some examples are:

- nuts, seeds and spices
- chickpeas and beans
- fermented veggies
- canned tomatoes
- coconut milk and cream
- rice, oats and quinoa
- mung bean fettuccine
- sauces and condiments
- tahini
- maple syrup.

Waste not, want not

Here in Australia, a scary amount of food is thrown into landfill each year. Aside from composting fruit and vegetables to make a nutrient-dense fertiliser for your garden, there are a few ways to avoid throwing out excess produce. If veggies are not fresh enough for a salad but still good enough to cook, I love to dice them all up, cover them with herbs, spices and some coconut aminos*, stir through some beans or chickpeas and roast them in the oven. Add some greens, avocado or hummus and fermented veg and you have yourself a yummy, nourishing bowl of goodness.

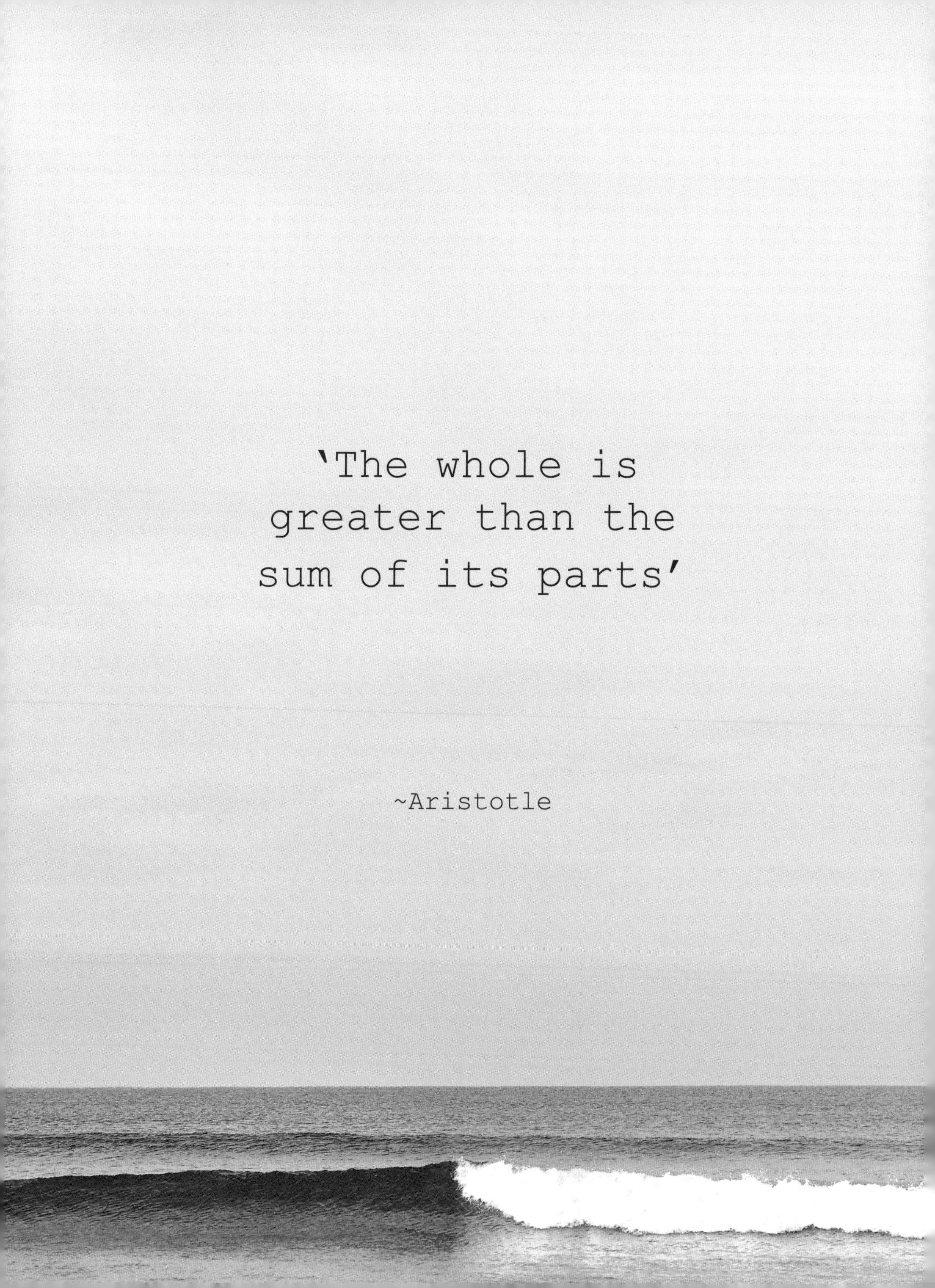

'The whole is
greater than the
sum of its parts'

~Aristotle

BREKKIE

EASY PANCAKES WITH
COCONUT YOGHURT & BERRIES

Pancakes. The old Sunday favourite. This simple version is the best of both worlds, just as yummy and satisfying yet made of nutrient-dense wholefoods. I love to serve them warm with berries and creamy coconut yoghurt. Oats are a great way to pack your breakfast with energy-giving good-quality carbohydrates. These pancakes freeze well and leftovers make a tasty snack topped with Nut-free chocky spread (see page 256) and fresh banana. You can replace the whole oats with wholemeal buckwheat flour if you have a sensitivity to oats.

Serves 2
Prep time: 5 minutes
Cook time: 25 minutes
Difficulty: Easy

PANCAKES

200 g (7 oz/2 cups) organic rolled
   (porridge) oats*

1 teaspoon baking powder

1 teaspoon ground cinnamon

1 teaspoon vanilla powder*

2 ripe ripe bananas, peeled

375 ml (12½ fl oz/1½ cups) plant-based
   milk*

TO SERVE

250 g (9 oz/1 cup) coconut yoghurt*

150 g (5½ oz/1 cup) frozen berries

Before you start, place the frozen berries in a bowl to thaw out while you prepare the pancakes.

For the pancakes, add the rolled oats, baking powder, cinnamon and vanilla powder to a food processor. Process on high speed until you have a flour-like consistency. Add the rest of the pancake ingredients and blend until smooth.

Heat a non-stick frying pan over low heat and spoon 1–2 tablespoons of the mixture into the pan for each pancake. Cook for 5 minutes or until small bubbles have formed on the surface of each pancake. Gently flip and cook the other sides.

Stack the pancakes and serve with the coconut yoghurt and berries. Enjoy.

BERRIES & CREAM
OATY RAW-NOLA BOWL

This super-easy recipe is a favourite of mine when I crave something sweet and sustaining in the morning. I like to top it with seasonal fruit - berries or mango are perfect in summer and poached pears or apples with cinnamon make a warming topping in winter. You can even add a little cacao before processing to create a delicious chocolatey version. The oaty raw-nola is perfect to make in larger batches. You can even add the whole lot to a glass jar and take it on the go for an ideal, filling brekkie or snack.

Serves 2
Prep time: 5 minutes
Difficulty: Very easy

OATY RAW-NOLA

200 g (7 oz/2 cups) organic rolled
  (porridge) oats*

1 teaspoon ground cinnamon

1 teaspoon vanilla powder*

10 medjool dates*, pitted

TO SERVE

250 g (9 oz/1 cup) coconut yoghurt*

125 g (4½ oz) berries

Add all the oaty raw-nola ingredients to a food processor and pulse until the mixture begins to stick together.

Spoon into two serving bowls, add the coconut yoghurt and scatter with the berries. You can also shape the mixture into balls for a perfect, yummy snack.

Store the raw-nola mixture in an airtight glass jar in the fridge for up to 1 week.

PURPLE SWEET POTATO
SMOOTHIE BOWL

No hard-to-find superfood powders in this recipe! The steamed purple sweet potato in this creamy breakfast bowl gives it the most beautiful colour and dreamy texture. Not only that, the purple sweet potato, which is white on the outside and purple on the inside, is an absolute powerhouse of nutrition. Combined with probiotic-rich coconut yoghurt, antioxidant-rich berries, fibre-packed oats and vitamin C-drenched lime, you have yourself one epic brekkie. Did I mention that it is delicious? I love making it for friends and family and asking them to guess the ingredients.

Serves 1
Prep time: 10 minutes
Cook time: 10 minutes
Difficulty: Easy

SMOOTHIE
225 g (8 oz) purple sweet potatoes*,
    peeled and diced
2 frozen ripe bananas
60 g (2 oz/¼ cup) coconut yoghurt*
juice of 1 lime

TOPPINGS
½ cup Oaty raw-nola (see page 26)
15 g (½ oz/¼ cup) shredded coconut
35 g (1¼ oz/¼ cup) frozen berries

Steam the sweet potato until soft. Set aside to cool.

Break the frozen bananas into chunks and add them to a blender or food processor with the coconut yoghurt, lime juice and sweet potato. Pulse to combine and blend until smooth.

Pour into a bowl, add the toppings and serve straight away.

LEMON 'RICOTTA' PANCAKES WITH BAKED BLUEBERRIES & APPLE

These pancakes are my favourite sweet brekkie to make when we are camping. I pre-prepare a big batch of the dry ingredients so it is easy to hand-mix the coconut yoghurt and mashed banana into it. It makes it slightly more rustic, but no less delicious! Nutritional yeast, sometimes called savoury yeast flakes, is an inactive yeast that provides the mild 'cheesy' flavour for this recipe without the dairy. The result is delicious and contains loads of vitamins and minerals, including B vitamins.

Serves 1
Prep time: 5 minutes
Cook time: 30 minutes
Difficulty: Easy

PANCAKES

100 g (3½ oz/1 cup) organic rolled (porridge) oats*
1 tablespoon nutritional yeast*
1 teaspoon baking powder
1 pinch salt
125 g (4½ oz/½ cup) coconut yoghurt*
zest and juice of 1 lemon
2 fresh or frozen ripe bananas

TO SERVE

75 g (2¾ oz/½ cup) fresh or frozen blueberries
½ granny smith apple (or other tart apple), thinly sliced
1 teaspoon lemon zest
1 tablespoon maple syrup*

Preheat the oven to 200°C (400°F) fan-forced and line a baking tray with baking paper. If you are camping, stoke your fire and let it burn down to medium heat. Place a frying pan over the fire.

Place the blueberries on the tray in the oven for about 20 minutes – or add to your frying pan if camping. Stir and cook until most of the moisture is absorbed.

Meanwhile, for the pancakes, combine the oats, nutritional yeast, baking powder and salt in a food processor. Process until a flour is formed.

Add the coconut yoghurt, lemon juice and banana to the food processor. Pulse to combine and blend until smooth. Or mash the banana and stir it into the dry ingredients with the coconut yoghurt and lemon juice. Stir in the lemon zest.

Heat a non-stick frying pan over low heat. Spoon 2 tablespoons of the mixture into the frying pan and cook until small bubbles appear, before flipping and repeating on the other side.

Stack the pancakes on a serving plate and top with the baked blueberries, sliced apple, lemon zest and a drizzle of maple syrup. Enjoy!

DREAMY TURKISH DELIGHT
COCONUT PORRIDGE

This delicious, creamy porridge is a perfect lazy brekkie and can be enjoyed hot or cold. If you don't have organic porridge oats available, it is easy to make your own. Simply put your whole oats in a food processor and pulse a few times. The delicious chocolate tahini sauce is my favourite way to top it but you can play around and use any fruits that are in season. Peaches, mango, sliced banana and berries are all delicious additions.

Serves 2
Prep time: 5 minutes (+ soaking time)
Difficulty: Very easy

PORRIDGE
200 g (7 oz/2 cups) organic rolled (porridge) oats*
750 ml (25½ fl oz/3 cups) plant-based milk* (I use coconut milk)
2 teaspoons food-grade rosewater

CHOCOLATE SAUCE
1 tablespoon hulled tahini*
1 teaspoon cacao powder*
2 teaspoons maple syrup*
1 tablespoon water

TO SERVE
1 tablespoon crushed pistachio nuts
2 teaspoons dried rose petals

Combine the porridge ingredients in a bowl. Stir to combine, then leave to soak for a few minutes or overnight in the fridge.

Whisk the chocolate sauce ingredients together and drizzle over the porridge. Top with the crushed pistachio nuts and dried rose petals.

To enjoy warm, simply place the soaked porridge ingredients in a small saucepan over low heat, stirring until warmed. Add the toppings and serve.

BREKKIE
BIKKIES THREE WAYS

These bikkies are the ultimate breakfast in a biscuit (cookie). They are full
of balanced wholefood goodness thanks to the oats, which are a rich source
of iron, fibre, magnesium and zinc as well as being higher in protein and
fat than many other grains. I like to throw a batch together at the start
of the week, not only because it means we are sorted for snacks and brekkies
on the run, but also because baking them makes the house smell incredible!
My absolute favourite way to enjoy them would have to be on the beach,
hot cuppa in hand, after a surf with a bunch of friends. Heaven.

Makes about 12 bikkies
Prep time: 5 minutes
Cook time: 15 minutes
Difficulty: Very easy

BLUEBERRY
& COCONUT

200 g (7 oz/2 cups) organic rolled
   (porridge) oats*
2 ripe bananas, peeled
2 tablespoons hulled tahini*
¼ teaspoon salt
1 teaspoon baking powder
1 teaspoon vanilla powder*
15 g (½ oz/¼ cup) shredded coconut
4 medjool dates*, pitted
75 g (2¾ oz/½ cup) fresh or frozen
   blueberries

GINGER
& SPICE

200 g (7 oz/2 cups) organic rolled (porridge)
   oats*
2 ripe bananas, peeled
2 tablespoons hulled tahini*
¼ teaspoon salt
1 teaspoon baking powder
1 tablespoon minced fresh ginger
2 teaspoons ground cinnamon
4 medjool dates*, pitted

$\rightarrow$

DOUBLE
CHOC CHIP

_____

200 g (7 oz/2 cups) organic rolled
　　(porridge) oats*
2 ripe bananas, peeled
2 tablespoons hulled tahini*
¼ teaspoon salt
1 teaspoon baking powder
1 teaspoon vanilla powder*
2 teaspoons cacao powder*
4 medjool dates*, pitted
2 tablespoons cacao nibs*

_____

Preheat the oven to 180°C (350°F) fan-forced and line a large baking tray
with baking paper.

Add all the ingredients to a food processor, except the cacao nibs
or blueberries. Pulse to combine and blend until the mixture becomes
a smooth dough.

Stir in the cacao nibs or blueberries. Roll the mixture into balls and space
them evenly across the prepared tray. Press down gently on each.

Bake for 12-15 minutes or until golden brown. Enjoy warm or store in the
fridge for up to 1 week.

SIMPLE CHIA &
BERRY PUDDING

This pared-back breakfast recipe is so easy to make and such a good option as a take-to-work brekkie. It transports so well and tastes and looks as good as it did when you first made it. All the ingredients are easy to come by and it is super gentle on the digestive system. Chia seeds, although small, deliver huge nutritional value. They are brimming with dietary fibre, omega-3, calcium and magnesium. The perfect base ingredient for your brekkie on the go!

Serves 1
Prep time: 10 minutes
Difficulty: Very easy

PUDDING

2 tablespoons chia seeds*

250 ml (8½ fl oz/1 cup) plant-based milk*
  (I use coconut milk)

¼ teaspoon vanilla powder*

TOPPINGS

50 g (1¾ oz/⅓ cup) fresh or frozen berries

1 teaspoon coconut flakes (optional)

Combine all the pudding ingredients in a jar. Place the lid on and shake well.

Leave to stand for 10 minutes before shaking again. Place in the fridge overnight for a quick breakfast the next morning or leave for another 10 minutes.

Lightly mash the berries. Spoon a little into the bottom of another glass jar. Top with some of the chia pudding and repeat these steps until all the pudding and berries are gone. Top with the coconut flakes and place a lid on the jar to take on the go or enjoy at home.

PERFECT AVO
ON OATY SEED TOAST

When it comes to avocado on toast, I think the perfect piece has just the right ratio of avo to toast. The other little bits and pieces you add can make or break the final product. I have had a few wins and a few losses over time. This simple combination is by far my favourite to date. It's all in the balance of salty, sweet, tangy, spicy, crunchy and creamy. I hope you love it too! If you haven't whipped up an easy batch of the Oaty seed loaf from page 254, never fear, a great-quality store-bought bread will also do the trick. Look for minimal ingredients and no numbers in the ingredients list.

Makes 2 pieces
Prep time: 5 minutes
Cook time: 5 minutes
Difficulty: Very easy

TOAST

2 slices Oaty seed loaf (see page 254)

½ avocado

juice of 1 lemon

1 tablespoon almonds, toasted

1 tablespoon sliced spring onions
   (scallions)

½ teaspoon chilli flakes

TO SERVE

2 tablespoons sauerkraut*

1 teaspoon balsamic vinegar or glaze

Toast two slices of oaty seed loaf. Mash the avocado well. Add half of the lemon juice and stir through. Roughly chop the almonds.

Divide the avocado mixture over the toast slices and sprinkle with the spring onion, toasted almonds, chilli flakes and the remainder of the lemon juice.

Serve with the sauerkraut and balsamic vinegar. Voila. The perfect simple brekkie.

SPICY TOFU SCRAMBLE

On a big camping adventure in beautiful Tassie we devoured this delicious meal almost every second day. It is tasty and guaranteed to leave you satisfied – especially when served with a few slices of my oaty seed loaf from page 254. It's a great way to start your day with some delicious, nourishing veggies, hearty bread and creamy avocado. We also enjoy the scramble in a wrap for lunch and as a bowl with rice and extra veg for dinner. The sky is the limit for one of my favourite and oh-so simple dishes.

Serves 2
Prep time: 5 minutes
Cook time: 10 minutes
Difficulty: Easy

SCRAMBLE

1 red onion, peeled and diced

1 red capsicum (bell pepper), diced

180 g (6½ oz/2 cups) mushrooms, sliced

200 g (7 oz) firm tofu*

1 teaspoon curry powder

2 teaspoons smoked paprika*

30 g (1 oz/½ cup) parsley, chopped

2 tablespoons chopped chives

TO SERVE

4 slices Oaty seed loaf (see page 254)

1 avocado, sliced

1 tablespoon balsamic vinegar or glaze

1 teaspoon parsley

1 teaspoon chives

Heat a non-stick frying pan over low heat, add the onion, red capsicum and mushrooms. Stir, then place a lid on the pan and cook for a few minutes.

Meanwhile, drain and rinse the tofu, crumble it into small pieces and add it to a fresh pan with the spices, stirring well. Increase the heat to medium and cook through.

Add the parsley and chives. Stir well and turn the heat off.

Toast the bread, top two slices with avocado, balsamic vinegar and herbs. Top the other two slices with tofu scramble and serve. Enjoy!

HERBY BREAKFAST
HASH BROWNS

This recipe came about when I was all out of bread and felt like good old avo on toast. The result was so good I just had to share it. The hash browns, dill and avocado are a perfect combination. I love to sneak a bit of fermented veg into meals where I can, and it complements this dish perfectly. This recipe also works really well with sweet potato, and leftovers are delicious when added to salads. If it's a simple and tasty savoury breakfast you are after, give this one a crack.

Serves 2
Prep time: 10 minutes
Cook time: 20 minutes
Difficulty: Easy

HASH BROWNS

200 g (7 oz) potatoes, washed and grated

½ onion, thinly sliced

1 tablespoon finely chopped dill

1 teaspoon garlic powder

¼ teaspoon salt

TO SERVE

½ avocado, sliced

2 tablespoons sauerkraut*

¼ teaspoon freshly ground black pepper

¼ teaspoon chilli flakes

1 tablespoon coconut aminos*

1 dill sprig (optional)

1 lemon or lime, quartered

Preheat the oven to 200°C (400°F) fan-forced. Line a large baking tray with baking paper.

Start by combining the potato, onion, dill, garlic powder and salt in a bowl and mix well.

Separate the mixture into about six portions. Mould into balls using your hands. Place on the tray and gently press each hash brown down with a spatula.

Place in the oven to bake for 20 minutes.

Top with sliced avocado and sauerkraut. Sprinkle all over with black pepper, chilli flakes, coconut aminos and dill (if using).

Serve with wedges of lemon or lime.

COMFORTING BAKED BEANS
WITH SMOKY COCONUT 'BACON'

On a crisp and cool morning nothing beats a hot brekkie. Best cooked over an open fire in the great outdoors to give them that extra-smoky quality, yet just as delicious made at home on a lazy Sunday morning, these beans also make a pretty delicious and quick weeknight dinner served with brown rice or roast spuds. The key is to find the juiciest, ripest cherry tomatoes you can and combine those with the freshest home-grown herbs. I like to serve them on toasted Oaty seed loaf (see page 254) with some creamy avocado.

Serves 2
Prep time: 5 minutes
Cook time: 30 minutes
Difficulty: Easy

BAKED BEANS

300 g (10½ oz) cherry tomatoes

1 red onion, peeled and diced

2 garlic cloves, minced

1 tablespoon coconut aminos*

250 g (9 oz) canned cannellini (lima) beans, drained and rinsed

½ teaspoon smoked paprika*

½ teaspoon chilli powder

½ teaspoon salt

½ teaspoon freshly ground black pepper

juice of ½ lemon

30 g (1 oz/1 cup) flat-leaf (Italian) parsley, chopped

TO SERVE

4 slices Oaty seed loaf (see page 254)

½ avocado, thickly sliced

2 tablespoons Smoky coconut 'bacon' (see page 278)

1 tablespoon chopped flat-leaf (Italian) parsley

Heat a saucepan over low heat – or if camping, over the fire. Add the whole cherry tomatoes, place the lid on the pan and leave to cook for about 5 minutes or until soft, stirring occasionally.

Add the onion, garlic and coconut aminos and sauté until translucent.

Add the cannellini beans, spices, salt, pepper and lemon juice. Stir well.

Simmer for a few minutes before adding the chopped parsley. Turn the heat off or remove from the fire and stir well.

Spoon the baked beans into two bowls and serve with toasted slices of oaty seed loaf, thick slices of avocado, smoky coconut 'bacon' and extra parsley.

Enjoy!

SPICED CHICKPEA PANCAKE
WITH MINTED YOGHURT

This scrumptious, fluffy, savoury pancake is a favourite of ours to make on camping adventures as it is so easy to cook over an open fire or on the camp stove. We don't only enjoy it as a breakfast either. It makes a delicious easy lunch, dinner or side dish. The pancake is best served straight away and the minted coconut yoghurt is the perfect addition to balance out the spice.

Makes 1 large pancake
Prep time: 5 minutes
Cook time: 10 minutes
Difficulty: Easy

PANCAKE
80 g (2¾ oz/¾ cup) chickpea flour
   (besan)*
1 teaspoon garam masala
½ teaspoon garlic powder
½ teaspoon baking powder
½ teaspoon ground turmeric
¼ teaspoon salt
zest and juice of ½ lemon
2 button mushrooms, finely diced

TO SERVE
60 g (2 oz/¼ cup) coconut yoghurt*
juice of ½ lemon
¼ teaspoon garlic powder
1 tablespoon chopped mint
1 teaspoon maple syrup*
1 tablespoon chopped chives
75 g (2¾ oz) cherry tomatoes, diced
½ avocado, sliced
1 teaspoon chilli flakes (optional)

Heat a non-stick frying pan over low heat.

Whisk all the dry pancake ingredients together with the lemon zest. Add 185 ml (6 fl oz/¾ cup) of water and the lemon juice. Whisk well to combine.

Add the chopped mushrooms and mix well.

Pour into the frying pan and cook for about 5 minutes on either side.

Whisk together the coconut yoghurt, lemon juice, garlic powder, chopped mint and maple syrup.

Serve the pancake topped with the minted coconut yoghurt, chopped chives, cherry tomatoes, sliced avocado and chilli flakes.

BOWLS

QUINOA SUSHI BOWL
WITH STICKY GINGER TOFU

This is my deconstructed, wholefood version of a classic sushi roll. For something so simple, it definitely delivers on nourishment and taste. Protein- and fibre-rich quinoa is a delicious alternative to white refined rice and the coconut aminos are the perfect sweet-and-salty addition in place of common soy sauce. The liver-cleansing beetroot provides a refreshing twist and the easy-to-make pickled ginger tops it all off with a punchy flavour. Of course, no sushi is ever complete without a healthy dose of avocado and sesame seeds.

Serves 2
Prep time: 15 minutes
Cook time: 20 minutes
Difficulty: Easy

QUICK PICKLED GINGER
80 g (2¾ oz) fresh ginger, peeled and sliced
125 ml (4 fl oz/½ cup) apple-cider vinegar*
1 tablespoon maple syrup*

TOFU
120 g (4½ oz) firm tofu*, diced
1 tablespoon coconut aminos*
1 tablespoon minced fresh ginger

BOWL
200 g (7 oz/1 cup) quinoa, rinsed
½ ripe avocado, sliced
140 g (5 oz/1 cup) beetroot (beets), grated
25 g (1 oz/½ cup) chives, chopped
1 sheet organic nori*, torn
1 teaspoon black sesame seeds
1 teaspoon white sesame seeds
2 tablespoons coconut aminos*

Combine the quick pickled ginger ingredients in a jar. Shake to combine and set aside while you prepare the rest.

Add the quinoa and 250 ml (8½ fl oz/1 cup) of water to a small saucepan. Bring to the boil and reduce to a simmer. Simmer until all the water is absorbed.

Combine the tofu, coconut aminos and minced ginger in a bowl. Mix well to coat.

Heat a non-stick frying pan over low heat. Fry the tofu, turning every now and then until cooked.

Assemble the bowls starting with the cooked quinoa. Top with all the other ingredients and finish with a generous sprinkling of coconut aminos and the quick pickled ginger.

Store the pickled ginger in an airtight glass jar in the fridge for up to 2 weeks.

FIVE-MINUTE
NOURISH BOWL

When you are craving something green, nourishing and satisfying, give this recipe a go. I love it for its balanced flavours and earthy textures. You can make it using broccoli, cauliflower, romanesco or even a combination of the three. I have used my favourite spices and herbs in this dish. But use what you have on hand and what is in season. This bowl makes the most delicious quick lunch or dinner!

Serves 2
Prep time: 5 minutes
Cook time: 5 minutes
Difficulty: Very easy

BOWL

1 head (about 700 g/1 lb 9 oz) broccoli, cauliflower or romanesco
1 teaspoon ground turmeric
1 teaspoon ground cumin
3 garlic cloves, minced
75 g (2¾ oz) mushrooms, sliced
2 teaspoons thyme
2 tablespoons beetroot (beet) sauerkraut*
2 tablespoons Miso hummus (see page 266)

TO SERVE

1 tablespoon coconut aminos*
1 teaspoon fresh thyme
1 teaspoon flat-leaf (Italian) parsley

Heat a non-stick frying pan on low.

Pulse the broccoli, spices and half the garlic in a food processor until a rice-like texture is achieved. Transfer to the frying pan and sauté until warmed through.

In a separate pan sauté the mushrooms, thyme and the remaining garlic until cooked through.

Spoon the broccoli 'rice', mushrooms, sauerkraut and hummus into a bowl, sprinkle with the coconut aminos and fresh herbs and enjoy!

BROWN RICE SESAME CONGEE

I love taking traditional, classic, tried-and-true dishes and turning them into a plant-based, wholefood version that is just as delicious! Congee is a savoury rice porridge popular in many Asian countries, often served with side dishes. I have swapped the white rice for whole brown rice and the toppings for nourishing kimchi, herbs, chillies and delicious coconut aminos. The result is soothing, warming and gentle on the stomach. Living in Victoria, we tend to enjoy this dish more in the cooler months. I find it helps to warm you from the inside out. It's also a great one to slow cook over an open fire or pop in the slow cooker for a fuss-free meal later.

Serves 4
Prep time: 5 minutes
Cook time: 1½ hours
Difficulty: Easy

CONGEE

220 g (8 oz/1 cup) brown rice, rinsed well

6 garlic cloves, minced

1 tablespoon minced fresh ginger

180 g (6½ oz/2 cups) shiitake mushrooms, sliced

1 tablespoon white sesame seeds

TO SERVE

½ tablespoon black sesame seeds

½ tablespoon white sesame seeds

15 g (½ oz/½ cup) coriander (cilantro) leaves

30 g (1 oz/½ cup) spring onions (scallions), sliced

1 red chilli, seeded and sliced

60 ml (2 fl oz/¼ cup) coconut aminos*

2 tablespoons kimchi*

Heat a large saucepan over medium heat. Add the rice, 2.5 litres (85 fl oz/10 cups) of water, garlic and ginger. Bring to the boil, reduce to a simmer, cover and cook for 1 hour, stirring every now and then.

Remove the lid, add the mushrooms and continue to simmer for a further 30 minutes or until all the water is absorbed. Stir in the sesame seeds and scoop into bowls.

Serve topped with the extra sesame seeds, coriander, spring onion, sliced chilli and coconut aminos, and the kimchi on the side.

BBQ TEMPEH
BUDDHA BOWL

The smoky barbecued flavour of the tempeh in this bowl is so delicious. It is quick and easy to prepare, making it a great lunch option. If you don't have the time to whip up a batch of hummus, a good-quality, store-bought variety will do the trick. I always have greens and herbs growing in the garden as they are so easy to care for and grow in abundance. Any kind you have on hand will suit this dish. I love English spinach and red lettuce! The trick is to shred them nice and finely. You can find organic tempeh at most wholefood and health food stores. This recipe also works well as a wrap for a delicious takeaway lunch or dinner!

Serves 2
Prep time: 5 minutes
Cook time: 10 minutes
Difficulty: Very easy

BBQ TEMPEH

1 teaspoon garlic powder

1 teaspoon smoked paprika*

1 tablespoon coconut aminos*

100 g (3½ oz) organic tempeh*,
   sliced into strips

SALAD

2 tablespoons beetroot (beet)
   sauerkraut*

60 g (2 oz/1½ cups) greens of choice,
   shredded

2 tablespoons Miso hummus
   (see page 266)

TO SERVE

1 tablespoon dill

1 tablespoon flat-leaf (Italian) parsley

Combine the garlic powder, smoked paprika and coconut aminos in a bowl and whisk to combine. Slice the tempeh into strips and add it to the marinade. Mix gently and set aside while you prepare the rest.

Assemble the salad ingredients in bowls.

Heat a non-stick frying pan over medium heat and cook the tempeh strips on both sides until crispy.

Add to the serving bowls and cover in fresh herbs. Enjoy!

CHARRED CORN & FRESH SALSA BURRITO BOWL

When it comes to flavour, freshness and colour you really can't beat Mexican food. The salsa and creamy avocado, balanced with hearty whole grains is a winning combo in this easy-to-make dish. It is also a perfect one when you are cooking for a group. Add some corn tortillas and enjoy the components of this dish as delicious, fresh tacos. Leftovers make a satisfying take-to-work lunch the following day!

Serves 2
Prep time: 10 minutes
Cook time: 30 minutes
Difficulty: Easy

BOWL

200 g (7 oz/1 cup) long-grain brown rice, rinsed well

400 g (14 oz/2 cups) corn kernels

1 teaspoon smoked paprika*

1 avocado

juice of 1 lime

1 pinch salt

1 pinch freshly ground black pepper

TO SERVE

250 g (9 oz) canned black beans, drained and rinsed

1½ cups Fresh salsa (see page 268)

2 tablespoons Cashew 'parmesan' (see page 272)

1 tablespoon roughly chopped coriander (cilantro) leaves

1 lime, quartered

1 pinch smoked paprika*

Combine the rice and 625 ml (21 fl oz/ 2½ cups) of water in a saucepan. Bring to the boil, reduce the heat and let simmer until all the water is absorbed, stirring occasionally.

While the rice cooks, heat a non-stick frying pan over medium heat. Add the corn kernels and smoked paprika. Stir until lightly charred. Remove from the heat and set aside.

Mash the avocado, lime juice, salt and black pepper together.

When the rice is cooked through, assemble bowls with the black beans, rice, charred corn, mashed avocado and fresh salsa.

Sprinkle with the cashew 'parmesan' and coriander and serve with lime wedges and smoked paprika.

DELICIOUS
DAL BOWL

Dal is a traditional dish from the Indian subcontinent, usually made of steamed rice and a lentil soup. In different areas and elevations, it is made in myriad ways. I like to make mine thick and hearty, with a fresh squeeze of lemon at the end to really bring out the flavours. You only need the basics on hand to whip it up. It packs a nutritional punch thanks to the nourishing lentils, rich in soluble fibre, plus plenty of fresh ginger and turmeric with their amazing anti-inflammatory properties. It's also easy to digest and guaranteed to satisfy the grumbliest of tummies. I always make a full batch as the leftovers are very tasty toasted in a wrap. If you are not a fan of coriander (cilantro), swap it for parsley as it works just as well.

Serves 4
Prep time: 10 minutes
Cook time: 30 minutes
Difficulty: Easy

DAL

1 white onion, diced

1 tablespoon minced fresh ginger

3 garlic cloves, minced

1 teaspoon curry powder

1 teaspoon ground turmeric

1 teaspoon ground cumin

500 g (1 lb 2 oz/2 cups) red lentils, rinsed well

2 tablespoons chopped coriander (cilantro) leaves

1.25 litres (42 fl oz/5 cups) vegetable stock

juice of 1 lemon

BOWL

285 g (10 oz/1½ cups) wild rice, rinsed

200 g (7 oz) mushrooms, sliced

40 g (1½ oz/1 cup) micro greens or sprouts

Combine all the dal ingredients, except for the lemon juice, in a large saucepan. Bring to the boil and reduce to a simmer. Cover and cook for 30 minutes or so, stirring every now and then until the dal starts to thicken. Remove from the heat, then stir in the lemon juice.

In a separate saucepan, add the wild rice and 750 ml (25½ fl oz/3 cups) of water. Bring to the boil and reduce to a simmer. Simmer until all the water is absorbed.

Heat a non-stick frying pan and add the sliced mushrooms and a dash of water. Gently cook over low heat until softened and browned.

Assemble the dal bowls with the rice, dal and sautéed mushrooms. Top with a generous sprinkling of micro greens or sprouts.

SPICY SAGE
SMASHING PUMPKIN BOWL

There is something about the combination of sage and pumpkin (winter squash) that is just perfect, especially when roasted. I return to this recipe again and again. The healthy whole fats in the avocado, contrasted with the sweet, juicy beetroot (beets) are super satisfying, and the roasted pumpkin seeds make a tasty, crunchy topping as well as providing loads of magnesium and zinc for a healthy immune system. That's why, whenever I am cooking pumpkin, I like to save the seeds to roast and scatter over the top (see page 76).

Serves 2
Prep time: 15 minutes
Cook time: 30 minutes
Difficulty: Easy

SMASHING PUMPKIN

1 kg (2 lb 3 oz) pumpkin (winter squash), seeds saved

2 teaspoons tamari*

5 g (¼ oz/¼ cup) sage

1 teaspoon chilli flakes

4 garlic cloves, minced

1 tablespoon nutritional yeast*

2 tablespoons coconut aminos*

BOWL

1 avocado, halved lengthways

1 teaspoon black sesame seeds

1 teaspoon white sesame seeds

140 g (5 oz/1 cup) beetroot (beets), grated

35 g (1¼ oz/1 cup tightly packed) rocket (arugula)

1 tablespoon coconut aminos*

2 tablespoons bean sprouts

1 teaspoon dukkah

Preheat the oven to 200°C (400°F) fan-forced.

Rinse the pumpkin seeds, pat them dry and toss in the tamari. Spread on a baking paper-lined tray and roast for 15 minutes or until crisp and golden brown.

Peel and dice the pumpkin. Line another tray with baking paper. Spread the pumpkin, sage, chilli, garlic, nutritional yeast and coconut aminos on the tray and bake for 30 minutes.

Peel the avocado and remove the stone. Roll the avocado halves in the sesame seeds and assemble with the beetroot and rocket.

When the pumpkin is done, transfer it to a bowl and lightly mash it. Add to the serving bowls and finish with the coconut aminos, bean sprouts, dukkah and roasted pumpkin seeds.

GARLICKY WILD RICE
'GREENIE BOWL'

The rice in this recipe provides all the flavour, texture and substance to perfectly accompany loads of alkalising greens. Have fun choosing your favourite greens to add to this nourishing bowl of goodness and enjoy them with a squeeze of lime and a creamy avo. Perfect when you are craving that green goodness. This recipe also works really well with quinoa or brown rice.

Serves 2
Prep time: 5 minutes
Cook time: 20 minutes
Difficulty: Easy

GARLICKY RICE

190 g (6½ oz/1 cup) wild rice

1 tablespoon hulled tahini*

1 tablespoon coconut aminos*

½ teaspoon garlic powder

SALAD

45 g (1½ oz/1 cup) English spinach

1 small cucumber, thinly sliced

60 g (2 oz/1 cup) alfalfa sprouts

1 sheet organic nori*, shredded

40 g (1½ oz/1 cup) pea shoots

1 avocado, sliced

½ teaspoon black sesame seeds

½ teaspoon white sesame seeds

1 lime, halved

Place the rice in a medium saucepan with 500 ml (17 fl oz/2 cups) of water. Bring to the boil, reduce to a simmer, cover and cook until all the water is absorbed.

While the rice cooks, assemble your salad in two serving bowls.

Once the rice is cooked, stir through the tahini, coconut aminos and garlic powder, add to the salad bowls and serve.

MEXI
CHILLI BOWL

This yummy chilli bowl is brimming with nourishing and sustaining ingredients that provide you with a generous dose of essential dietary fibre and more than enough protein. It always hits the spot when you feel like a tasty meal in a hurry. The chilli freezes really well in portions, making it an ideal recipe for your Sunday food prep. I love to make more than needed and use the leftovers to top baked sweet potato, or to have in tacos, with rice, salad or charred corn. It is satisfying yet energising and doubles as a nice, cheap, easy meal to feed many.

Serves 2-4
Prep time: 5 minutes
Cook time: 30 minutes
Difficulty: Easy

CHILLI

1 onion, diced

3 garlic cloves, minced

2 red capsicums (bell peppers), diced

375 g (13 oz) canned tomatoes

280 g (10 oz) canned brown lentils, drained and rinsed

250 g (9 oz) canned kidney beans, drained and rinsed

1 red chilli, diced

2 teaspoons smoked paprika*

2 teaspoons ground cumin

½ teaspoon salt

BOWL

2 handfuls Corn tortilla chips (see page 172)

½ cup Fresh salsa (see page 268)

1 avocado, sliced

7 g (¼ oz/¼ cup) coriander (cilantro) leaves

handful watercress or sprouts

1 lime, quartered

Heat a large saucepan on low. Lightly sauté the onion, garlic and capsicum.

Add all the other chilli ingredients and stir well. Simmer for 30 minutes or until cooked through.

Spoon into bowls and serve with the tortilla chips, fresh salsa, sliced avocado, coriander, watercress or sprouts and a wedge of lime.

RAINBOW MACRO BOWL WITH
CRISPY TOFU & MISO SAUCE

This macro bowl has all the elements, colours and flavours of a balanced bowl of goodness. Whole grains, raw veggies, protein, fermented veg, tangy miso sauce and mineral-rich sea vegetables. It is a great way to use up veggies and a sure-fire hit when unexpected guests arrive at mealtimes. You can play with different combinations. I like to make a little extra dressing to keep in the fridge for a quick throw-together salad the next day. You can also use the same recipe in a wrap or nori sheet to take to work for lunch or a day at the beach. Swap the brown rice for quinoa, buckwheat or any other whole grain you like. Perfection.

Serves 2
Prep time: 10 minutes
Cook time: 20 minutes
Difficulty: Easy

TOFU

250 g (9 oz) organic firm tofu*, cubed

1 tablespoon coconut aminos*

BOWL

200 g (7 oz/1 cup) long-grain brown rice, washed

100 g (3½ oz) small zucchini (courgettes), grated

100 g (3½ oz) carrots, grated

100 g (3½ oz) beetroot (beets), grated

2 tablespoons sauerkraut*

1 sheet organic nori*, shredded

1 cup Tangy miso sauce (see page 276)

Cover the tofu with the coconut aminos and set aside to marinate.

Meanwhile, combine the rice and 500 ml (17 fl oz/2 cups) of water in a small saucepan and bring to the boil. Reduce to a simmer and cook until all the water is absorbed.

Heat a non-stick frying pan over medium heat before adding the marinated tofu. Cook until lightly browned on all sides, turning the pieces as you go.

Assemble your bowls starting with a base of brown rice, then top with the zucchini, carrot, sauerkraut, beetroot, nori, fried tofu and miso sauce before serving.

ROSEMARY SLOW-ROASTED PUMPKIN BOWL WITH TANGY MISO SAUCE

The rosemary roasted pumpkin (winter squash) in this recipe has so much flavour, especially when drizzled with Tangy miso sauce (see page 276). It makes tasty leftovers, especially when chopped and stirred through salads. Here is a tip for you: don't throw out your pumpkin seeds! Instead, rinse and drain them. Pat dry, toss in a little tamari or coconut aminos and roast for fifteen minutes or until crispy. They will be a yummy snack while you create the rest of your meal, or a scrumptious topping with a welcome crunch. Plus, they are a great dose of loads of goodies, such as zinc, magnesium and those amazing plant-based omega-3 fats. Waste not, want not.

Serves 2
Prep time: 10 minutes
Cook time: 1 hour
Difficulty: Easy

ROASTED PUMPKIN

1 kg (2 lb 3 oz) pumpkin (winter squash),
   seeds saved
2 tablespoons coconut aminos*
3 garlic cloves, sliced
10 g (¼ oz/¼ cup) rosemary sprigs,
   stalks removed
½ teaspoon salt

TO SERVE

200 g (7 oz/1 cup) black rice
40 g (1½ oz/2 cups loosely packed) rocket
   (arugula)
1 cup Tangy miso sauce (see page 276)

Preheat the oven to 180°C (350°F) fan-forced.

Wash the pumpkin seeds, pat them dry and toss in half of the coconut aminos. Place in the oven to roast while you prepare the rest of the dish.

Cut the pumpkin into wedges.

Line a tray with baking paper. Place the pumpkin on the tray. Brush the wedges with the remaining coconut aminos and sprinkle with garlic, rosemary and salt.

Place in the oven to bake for 1 hour or until soft and golden brown.

Rinse the rice well, then add it to a small saucepan with 500 ml (17 fl oz/ 2 cups) of water. Bring to the boil and reduce to a simmer for 15 minutes or until all the water is absorbed.

Assemble the pumpkin, rocket and rice in a bowl and drizzle over the miso sauce before serving.

SEEDED MUSTARD &
SWEET POTATO NOURISH BOWL

I think I could eat this meal every day. It feels like it satisfies on all levels: taste, spice, nutrients and ease. If you roast your sweet potatoes the night before it also makes a great lunch to take on the go the next day and is just as yummy cold. I like to top mine with Miso hummus (see page 266) but you could also add fermented veggies, pickles, olives and dukkah.

Serves 2
Prep time: 10 minutes
Cook time: 40 minutes
Difficulty: Easy

SWEET POTATO
800 g (1 lb 12 oz) sweet potato

1 tablespoon coconut aminos*

2 tablespoons seeded mustard

1 garlic clove, minced

¼ teaspoon salt

BOWL
1 large avocado

juice of ½ lime

2 tablespoons Miso hummus (see page 266)

40 g (1½ oz/2 cups loosely packed) rocket (arugula)

½ teaspoon freshly ground black pepper

1 lime, halved

Preheat the oven to 180°C (350°F) fan-forced.

Wash and dice the sweet potatoes.

Combine the coconut aminos, seeded mustard, garlic and salt in a large bowl. Whisk to combine. Add the sweet potatoes and mix well.

Transfer to a baking paper-lined tray and place in the oven to roast for 40 minutes.

Meanwhile, mash the avocado and mix in the lime juice.

Assemble the hummus and rocket in a bowl. Add the roasted sweet potato and sprinkle with the pepper. Serve with the lime halves.

SALADS

HERBY BLACK RICE SALAD WITH MINTED BEETROOT YOGHURT

If you are after a simple, crowd-pleasing salad recipe, this is it. You can double the recipe and serve it as a share plate or take it to work for lunch, packing the yoghurt dressing separately. The creamy, probiotic-rich minted beetroot (beet) dressing is the perfect contrast to the crunchy, herby salad and the colours are so divine. Black rice provides the bonus of extra antioxidants and vitamin E.

Serves 2
Prep time: 10 minutes
Cook time: 20 minutes
Difficulty: Easy

SALAD

30 g (1 oz/¼ cup) sunflower kernels

40 g (1½ oz/¼ cup) pine nuts

40 g (1½ oz/¼ cup) cup almonds

200 g (7 oz/1 cup) black rice, washed

½ red onion, finely diced

15 g (½ oz/¼ cup) dill, chopped

15 g (½ oz/¼ cup) parsley, chopped

2 tablespoons coconut aminos*

BEETROOT YOGHURT

250 g (9 oz/1 cup) coconut yoghurt*

45 g (1½ oz/⅓ cup) beetroot (beets), grated

juice of ½ lemon

1 tablespoon finely chopped mint

Heat a non-stick frying pan on low. Add the sunflower kernels, pine nuts and almonds and gently toast until golden. Set aside to cool.

Add the black rice and 500 ml (17 fl oz/ 2 cups) of water to a saucepan. Bring to the boil and simmer until all the water is absorbed. Set aside to cool.

Meanwhile, add the coconut yoghurt, beetroot and lemon juice to a blender or food processor and blend until smooth. Add the chopped mint and stir well. Spread the beetroot yoghurt mixture over two serving plates.

Combine all the salad ingredients and serve on top of the beetroot yoghurt.

TANGY THAI
KELP NOODLE SALAD

This salad is so tangy, fresh and creamy. It is like a fresher, lighter version of a pad thai with the added benefits of miso. Miso, originating in Japan, is rich in probiotics, aiding digestion and providing high-quality plant-based B vitamins. Combined with loads of fibre, vitamins and minerals from the fresh, crunchy veggies, here you have yourself one very healthy and tasty salad.

Serves 2
Prep time: 10 minutes
Difficulty: Very easy

SALAD

1 packet (12 oz/340 g) kelp noodles*

100 g (3½ oz) carrot, julienned

100 g (3½ oz) red capsicum (bell pepper), julienned

25 g (1 oz/½ cup) chives, chopped

10 g (¼ oz/⅓ cup) coriander (cilantro) leaves

½ cup Tangy miso sauce (see page 276)

TO SERVE

115 g (4 oz/¾ cup) cashew nuts, chopped

Place the kelp noodles in a bowl of cold water while you prepare the rest of the dish.

Heat a non-stick frying pan on low. Add the cashew nuts and lightly toast. Set aside to cool.

Drain the kelp noodles until no liquid remains.

Combine all the salad ingredients in a bowl and toss the miso sauce through. Scatter with the toasted cashew nuts and serve.

SPICED CHICKPEA 'CAESAR' SALAD

In this salad I have added spiced chickpeas instead of the traditional croutons. The rich dressing is replaced with a combination of plant-based ingredients that do not compromise on taste. I like to make a big batch of the dressing to have on hand as it is so delicious on any salad or as a mayonnaise substitute in a toasted sandwich. This is also such a great way to add loads of nutrient-dense kale to your meal in a tasty way. Kale is also a wonderful leafy green to grow yourself. Plant a few seedlings and you will not be visiting the store for a bunch any time soon, that's for sure.

Serves 2
Prep time: 10 minutes
Cook time: 10 minutes
Difficulty: Easy

SALAD
135 g (5 oz/3 cups) kale, finely shredded

75 g (23/4 oz/1 cup) red cabbage, shredded

1½ cups Spiced chickpeas (see page 270)

DRESSING
125 ml (4 fl oz/½ cup) plant-based milk*
   (I use almond milk)

3 tablespoons hulled tahini*

juice of 1 lemon

2 teaspoons maple syrup*

1 teaspoon garlic powder

1 pinch salt

Add all the dressing ingredients to a bowl and whisk to combine. Combine the kale and cabbage in a separate bowl and coat in three-quarters of the dressing.

Scatter the spiced chickpeas over the salad and drizzle the remaining dressing over the top before serving.

GRILLED ZUCCHINI, PEA, MINT & 'PARMESAN' SALAD

I love making this salad to go with pizzas. The flavours are so yummy and fresh, which I find complement pizza really well. It is also a goodie for a balmy summer's night when you feel like something light yet satisfying. I also make it when we are camping, as the zucchini (courgettes) and toasted almonds take on a smoky quality over an open fire that is just scrumptious. Zucchini grows really well through summer so, if you plant it early enough, you might find you have an abundance come the warmer months.

Serves 2
Prep time: 10 minutes
Cook time: 20 minutes
Difficulty: Easy

SALAD

2 large zucchini (courgettes), thinly sliced lengthways
80 g (2¾ oz/½ cup) almonds
155 g (5½ oz/1 cup) fresh peas
10 g (¼ oz/½ cup) mint leaves
1 tablespoon baby capers
2 teaspoons lemon zest

TO SERVE

2 tablespoons coconut aminos*
½ cup Cashew 'parmesan' (see page 272)

Heat a large chargrill pan over medium heat and grill the zucchini slices on both sides.

Roughly chop the almonds and toast on a hotplate over the fire or in a non-stick frying pan over medium heat.

Layer the grilled zucchini, peas, mint, capers, toasted almonds and lemon zest on a serving plate.

Drizzle with the coconut aminos and sprinkle with the cashew 'parmesan'.

TURMERIC-ROASTED CAULIFLOWER, POMEGRANATE & COCONUT SALAD

I love finding new ways to sneak anti-inflammatory turmeric into meals, drinks and even the odd dessert as a natural food colouring. This salad was inspired by Middle Eastern and Indian flavours and colours, and the creamy coconut yoghurt dressing complements it perfectly. It makes a great share plate and adds a welcome splash of colour to a lunch or dinner spread.

Serves 2 as a side dish
Prep time: 10 minutes
Cook time: 30 minutes
Difficulty: Easy

SALAD

1 teaspoon ground cumin

1 teaspoon ground turmeric

1 teaspoon chilli powder

juice of ½ lemon

1 tablespoon coconut aminos*

1 head (about 750 g/1 lb 11 oz)
    cauliflower

50 g (1¾ oz/⅓ cup) pine nuts

DRESSING

125 g (4½ oz/½ cup) coconut yoghurt*

½ teaspoon garlic powder

2 teaspoons maple syrup*

juice of 1 lemon

TO SERVE

1 large pomegranate

30 g (1 oz/1 cup) flat-leaf (Italian) parsley

1 pinch ground cumin

Preheat the oven to 200°C (400°F) fan-forced.

For the salad, stir the spices, lemon juice and coconut aminos together in a mixing bowl. Break the cauliflower into florets and toss in the spice mixture.

Line a baking tray with baking paper. Spread with the cauliflower florets and roast for about 30 minutes.

Heat a non-stick frying pan over low heat, add the pine nuts and lightly toast. Watch them as they can burn quickly.

Whisk the dressing ingredients together.

Assemble the salad ingredients on a plate and add generous dollops of the dressing. Remove the seeds from the pomegranate and sprinkle over the salad. Finish with the parsley and cumin.

CREAMY ROAST POTATO
& DILL SALAD

Traditional potato salad is a bit of a nostalgic dish for me and one of the reasons I wanted to come up with a completely dairy- and egg-free wholefood alternative. The result, I think, tastes even better. This salad has the same great comforting quality and the tangy mustard dressing is so simple to make. I have roasted the potatoes in this version as I like the extra crunch, but you could just as easily steam yours if you like. It's an all-round winner in my opinion and one you will want to contribute next time you are asked to bring a plate.

Serves 2
Prep time: 10 minutes
Cook time: 30 minutes
Difficulty: Easy

SALAD

1 kg (2 lb 3 oz) potatoes, washed
   and diced
1 red onion, diced
30 g (1 oz/½ cup) spring onions
   (scallions), sliced
handful dill, chopped
½ cup Smoky coconut 'bacon'
   (see page 278)

DRESSING

125 ml (4 fl oz/½ cup) plant-based milk*
   (I use almond milk)
4 tablespoons hulled tahini*
2 teaspoons miso*
½ teaspoon garlic powder
juice of ½ lemon
1 tablespoon seeded mustard

Preheat the oven to 200°C (400°F) fan-forced.

Line a tray with baking paper, spread the potato out on the tray and place in the oven to cook for 30 minutes or until crispy. Once cooked, set aside to cool.

To make your dressing, add all the ingredients, except for the seeded mustard, to a blender or food processor and blend until smooth. You can also use a fork to whisk the ingredients if you do not have a blender handy. Add the seeded mustard and stir until evenly combined.

Combine the potatoes and all the salad ingredients in a bowl. Add the dressing and mix well. Serve.

FRESH SUMMER
PASTA SALAD

One of the best things about this salad is that three of the main ingredients are easy to grow yourself over summer, so you can enjoy it many times over the season. I first discovered this combination when I was given a bunch of English spinach, basil and tomatoes from a friend's veggie garden and this is what I came up with. I highly recommend hunting down mung bean fettuccine at your local health food store too. I think it is the closest thing to regular pasta without the gluten. I actually prefer it. We make this salad over the warmer months when tomatoes are in season and have the most flavour.

Serves 2-4
Prep time: 5 minutes
Cook time: 10 minutes
Difficulty: Very easy

1 packet (250 g/9 oz) mung bean
  fettuccine*
225 g (8 oz) cherry tomatoes, halved
90 g (3 oz/2 cups) English spinach,
  chopped
30 g (1 oz/1 cup loosely packed) basil
125 g (4½ oz/1 cup) olives, pitted
½ cup Cashew 'parmesan' (see page 272)
3 tablespoons coconut aminos*

Bring a pot of water to the boil. Add the fettuccine, reduce to a simmer and cook for 5-6 minutes. Drain and gently rinse in cold water until the fettuccine is cool.

Stir in all the other ingredients and serve immediately.

If you want to prepare this dish to eat later, don't add the coconut aminos until serving.

SPICY SESAME & GINGER
BLACK BEAN NOODLE SALAD

Once, when I thought I would throw together a soba noodle salad to take to a dinner, I found that I was out of soba noodles with no time to visit the shops. So I tried substituting with black bean spaghetti instead. It turned out even better. The texture of the noodles is perfect. They hold their shape and the salad is still good the next day as leftovers. The flavours in this salad are really punchy and the hint of spice is divine.

Serves 2
Prep time: 10 minutes
Cook time: 10 minutes
Difficulty: Easy

DRESSING

1 tablespoon coconut aminos*

½ teaspoon garlic powder

1 tablespoon miso*

zest and juice of 1 lime

2 teaspoons minced fresh ginger

SALAD

1 tablespoon white sesame seeds

1 tablespoon black sesame seeds

1 packet (200 g/7 oz) black bean
   spaghetti*

100 g (3½ oz/1 cup) sugar snap peas,
   halved lengthways

30 g (1 oz/½ cup) spring onions
   (scallions), sliced

1 large red chilli, diced

15 g (½ oz/½ cup) coriander (cilantro)
   leaves

Heat a non-stick frying pan over medium heat and lightly toast the sesame seeds.

Whisk the dressing ingredients together.

Bring 1 litre (34 fl oz/4 cups) of water to the boil. Add the black bean spaghetti and simmer for about 8 minutes. Once cooked, drain and rinse in cold water.

Transfer the spaghetti to a large salad bowl and add all the other ingredients. Toss until well combined and enjoy.

If you are taking this on the go, store the salad and dressing separately.

INSALATA CAPRESE
WITH 'NOTZZARELLA'

Insalata caprese, or 'salad of Capri', is traditionally a simple salad made of sliced mozzarella, tomatoes, basil, salt, pepper and olive oil. I have switched the olive oil for fermented coconut aminos (which gives it such a great flavour) and dairy mozzarella for my plant-based version (see page 260).
This is such a perfect, fresh summer salad using ingredients that can be readily available in your veggie garden. The quality of the tomatoes you use makes all the difference. Vine ripened is best and organic is even better.

Serves 2
Prep time: 5 minutes
Difficulty: Very easy

SALAD

225 g (8 oz) cherry tomatoes, halved

2 vine-ripened tomatoes, sliced

15 g (½ oz/½ cup loosely packed) basil

90 g (3 oz/¾ cup) black olives, pitted

½ cup 'Cashew notzzarella' (see
 page 260)

TO SERVE

2 tablespoons coconut aminos*

1 teaspoon freshly ground black pepper

Arrange the salad ingredients on two platters or one big share plate.

Top with the coconut aminos and cracked pepper. Serve immediately.

EPIC SWEET SPUD SALAD
WITH MISO HUMMUS

The sweet potato is one amazing vegetable. It is rich in so many nutrients including vitamin C, manganese, copper and B6 as well as potassium and vitamin A. Sweet potatoes suit almost every meal and add such a tasty and substantial element to salads and nourish bowls. This salad is an old favourite of mine and I have been making it for years. It makes a really tasty packed lunch or substantial salad contribution to a beach picnic. Whenever or wherever it is enjoyed, it is always perfect.

Serves 2-4
Prep time: 10 minutes
Cook time: 30 minutes
Difficulty: Easy

BAKED SWEET POTATO

1 kg (2 lb 3 oz) sweet potato, peeled
   and diced
juice of 1 lemon
1 tablespoon oregano, fresh or dried
2 teaspoons garlic powder

SALAD

140 g (5 oz/1 cup) beetroot (beets),
   grated
40 g (1½ oz/2 cups loosely packed) rocket
   (arugula)
125 g (4½ oz/1 cup) olives, pitted

TO SERVE

4 tablespoons Miso hummus
   (see page 266)

Preheat the oven to 220°C (430°F) fan-forced.

Line a large baking tray with baking paper. Spread the sweet potato evenly across the tray. Sprinkle with the lemon juice, oregano and garlic powder. Gently stir, then place in the oven for 30 minutes.

Assemble and toss the salad mixture together, add the roast sweet potato and serve with a generous dollop of hummus.

FALAFEL CRUMBLE SALAD
WITH PICKLED ONION

When I have leftover falafel I like to crumble them and enjoy them over salad. So why not skip the rolling and moulding part of the process and make a crumble instead? This crumble is full of all the protein and flavour of a traditional falafel with even more of the crunch. It adds so much texture and flavour as a salad topping. The whole recipe is also perfect enjoyed as a wrap, and leftovers make a tasty lunch or share plate.

Serves 2
Prep time: 10 minutes
Cook time: 25 minutes
Difficulty: Easy

FALAFEL CRUMBLE

250 g (9 oz) canned chickpeas, drained and rinsed

1 tablespoon hulled tahini*

30 g (1 oz/½ cup) parsley, finely chopped

juice of ½ lemon

1 tablespoon coconut aminos*

½ teaspoon ground cumin

¼ teaspoon salt

SALAD

120 g (2 oz/2 cups) parsley, chopped

225 g (8 oz) cherry tomatoes, diced

60 g (2 oz/½ cup) olives, pitted

½ cup Quick pickled onion (see page 264)

TO SERVE

1 cup Miso hummus (see page 266)

Preheat the oven to 200°C (400°F) fan-forced. Line a baking tray with baking paper.

Lightly mash the chickpeas with a fork. Add all the other crumble ingredients and stir well.

Spread the crumble ingredients out on the prepared tray. Bake for 25 minutes, stirring after 10 minutes.

Once the crumble is cooked, combine the salad ingredients, sprinkle with the crumble and serve with a generous helping of miso hummus.

ZINGY KALE & QUINOA SALAD
WITH SPICY CANDIED WALNUTS

As you probably already know, kale is an absolute powerhouse of nutrients, including iron and calcium. It also grows like crazy and a few plants will give you an abundance of the crisp, edible leaves. Any variety works well in this salad. The finer you shred the kale the better. With spicy, salty and sweet candied walnuts, quinoa and creamy white bean pesto it makes the perfect hearty salad.

Serves 2
Prep time: 10 minutes
Cook time: 20 minutes
Difficulty: Easy

SALAD
200 g (7 oz/1 cup) quinoa, washed

500 ml (17 fl oz/2 cups) vegetable stock

4 tablespoons coconut aminos*

75 g (2¾ oz/¾ cup) walnuts, halved

90 g (3 oz/2 cups) kale, stalks removed

125 g (4½ oz/1 cup) olives, pitted and
   halved

juice of 1 lemon

TO SERVE
1 cup White bean pesto (see page 262)

1 lemon, halved (optional)

Combine the quinoa and vegetable stock in a saucepan and bring to the boil. Reduce to simmer until all the liquid is absorbed. Set aside to cool.

Heat a non-stick frying pan on low, add 2 tablespoons of the coconut aminos and the walnuts. Lightly toast until all the liquid is absorbed. Set aside to cool.

Finely shred the kale. Combine all the salad ingredients in a bowl and coat with the lemon juice and the remainder of the coconut aminos. Serve with the white bean pesto and lemon halves, if desired.

FRESH TACO SALAD
IN A TOASTED EDIBLE BOWL

This crispy edible bowl filled with a fresh and hearty Mexican-style salad is such a great way to pack in the veggies and a variety of colour. It is usually on the menu at our house when I feel like something fresh and easy. It always delivers on flavour and texture. The edible bowl is so easy to make and provides a welcome crunch.

Serves 2
Prep time: 10 minutes
Cook time: 10 minutes
Difficulty: Easy

BOWL
4 mountain bread wraps
1 lemon or lime, halved

SALAD
kernels from 1 corn cob
250 g (9 oz) canned black beans, drained
  and rinsed
25 g (1 oz/½ cup) coriander (cilantro),
  chopped, plus extra to serve
1 red capsicum (bell pepper), finely diced
75 g (2¾ oz/1 cup) red cabbage, finely
  shredded
15 g (½ oz/¼ cup) spring onions
  (scallions), thinly sliced
2 tablespoons coconut aminos*
1 avocado
1 lime, halved

Preheat the oven to 200°C (400°F) fan-forced.

Gently press two wraps into each of two round ovenproof dishes, placing the second wrap on the diagonal so the four points face in different directions. Sprinkle with the lemon or lime juice and bake for 10 minutes. Remove and set aside to cool.

Heat a non-stick frying pan over low heat. Add the corn kernels and lightly char.

Combine all the salad ingredients, except the avocado and lime, in a bowl and toss together. Mash the avocado in a separate bowl.

Spoon the salad mixture into the baked wrap shells and top with the mashed avocado. Sprinkle with extra coriander and serve with the lime halves.

MAINS

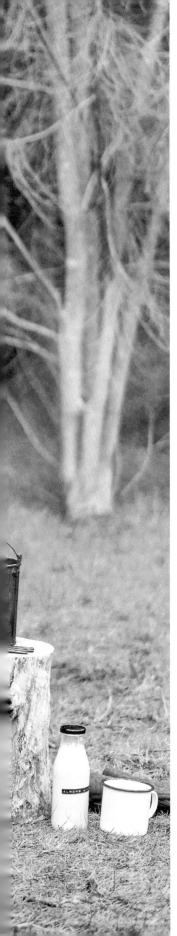

MIDDLE EASTERN
STUFFED EGGPLANTS

When I first made this dish for Frase, he was blown away by the flavours. It may take a little longer than most of the other recipes in this book but it is well worth the effort. The fresh, herby yoghurt dressing paired with the spicy, nutty and savoury stuffing in a crispy eggplant (aubergine) skin is just magic. This recipe is best enjoyed straight away, but any leftover stuffing freezes well and is also yummy rolled into balls and baked.

Serves 4
Prep time: 10 minutes
Cook time: 50 minutes
Difficulty: Medium

STUFFED EGGPLANTS

2 large eggplants (aubergines)

½ head cauliflower florets
  (about 200 g/7 oz)

300 g (10½ oz) mushrooms, sliced

50 g (1¾ oz/½ cup) walnuts

1 onion, diced

70 g (2½ oz/½ cup) dried cranberries

½ teaspoon salt

1½ teaspoons ground cumin

YOGHURT DRESSING

185 g (6½ oz/¾ cup) coconut yoghurt*

1 tablespoon chopped mint

1 tablespoon chopped coriander
  (cilantro) leaves

juice of ½ lemon

1 teaspoon maple syrup*

½ teaspoon garlic powder

TO SERVE

1 tablespoon chopped coriander
  (cilantro) leaves

1 tablespoon mint

seeds of 1 pomegranate

2 tablespoons pine nuts, toasted

1 lime, quartered

Preheat the oven to 180°C (350°F) fan-forced.

Slice the eggplants lengthways and scoop out the flesh, saving it for the stuffing. Place the halves, skin side down, on a baking paper-lined tray. Bake in the oven for 20 minutes while you prepare the rest of the dish.

To make the stuffing, add the reserved eggplant flesh, cauliflower florets, mushrooms and walnuts to a food processor and pulse until you get a rice-like consistency. Heat a non-stick frying pan. Combine the eggplant mixture, onion, cranberries, salt and cumin in a frying pan. Cook the mixture over low heat for about 20 minutes, stirring every few minutes.

Remove the eggplant skins from the oven and stuff the eggplants with the cooked mixture. Return to the oven to bake for a further 30 minutes.

Combine the dressing ingredients in a small bowl and whisk together.

Once the eggplants are done, drizzle with the yoghurt dressing and scatter with the extra fresh herbs, pomegranate seeds and toasted pine nuts. Serve with a few wedges of lime.

BEETROOT &
DILL BORSCHT

Borscht is a traditional eastern European soup. I have given it bit of a fresh twist and the result is nourishing and full of flavour. Beetroot (beet) is such a powerful detoxifier as well as a nutrient powerhouse, not to mention versatile. Just look at that colour! You can't help but feel virtuous just making this soup. I find it a great option to use some of those spring harvest veggies and a warming soup is just the thing when the early mornings here in southern Victoria are still a tad on the chilly side.

Serves 4
Prep time: 10 minutes
Cook time: 45 minutes
Difficulty: Easy

SOUP

1 onion, peeled and diced

1 tablespoon minced fresh ginger

1 litre (34 fl oz/4 cups) vegetable stock

700 g (1 lb 9 oz) beetroot (beets), peeled and diced

250 g (9 oz) parsnips, washed and diced

250 g (9 oz) canned cannellini (lima) beans, drained and rinsed

15 g (½ oz/¼ cup) dill, finely chopped

2 tablespoons apple-cider vinegar*

2 tablespoons coconut aminos*

TO SERVE

2 tablespoons coconut yoghurt*

1 tablespoon chopped dill

Heat a large saucepan over low heat. Sauté the onion and ginger with a splash of vegetable stock until translucent.

Add all the other soup ingredients, except for the coconut aminos. Stir well, bring to the boil and reduce to a simmer for about 40 minutes or until the beetroot and parsnips have softened.

Turn the heat off and add the coconut aminos.

Using a hand-held blender, process the soup to your desired consistency. Serve with the coconut yoghurt and sprinkle over the dill.

MUSHROOM
'NEAT-BALL' PASTA

Have an abundance of mushrooms on hand? Conjuring up some of these yummy 'neat-balls' is a perfect way to use them. This simple recipe makes the most amazingly flavoured and textured meatballs - without the meat. You can combine them with any pasta you like. I love to use either mung bean fettuccine or brown rice penne. Even spiralised zucchini (courgette) noodles make a great addition. You can also use the same recipe to make larger portions into hearty burger patties to go with a colourful salad.

Serves 2-4 (makes about 20 balls)
Prep time: 20 minutes
Cook time: 30 minutes
Difficulty: Medium

BALLS
350 g (12½ oz) mushrooms, finely diced
1 onion, peeled and finely diced
75 g (2¾ oz/¾ cup) walnuts
20 g (¾ oz/⅓ cup) nutritional yeast*
1 teaspoon chilli flakes
60 g (2 oz/1 cup) parsley, roughly
    chopped
1 pinch of salt

SAUCE
400 g (14 oz) canned diced tomatoes
2 tablespoons chopped parsley
1 garlic clove, minced
1 tablespoon coconut aminos*

TO SERVE
1 packet (200 g/7 oz) mung bean
    fettuccine*
2 tablespoons Cashew 'parmesan'
    (see page 272)
1 tablespoon oregano leaves

Preheat the oven to 200°C (400°F) fan-forced and heat a non-stick frying pan over medium heat. Fry the mushrooms and onion, stirring until most of the liquid has evaporated, then set aside. Add the walnuts, nutritional yeast, chilli flakes, parsley and salt to a food processor. Pulse a few times. Add the cooked mushroom and onion. Pulse a few times until the mixture is evenly combined and begins to stick together.

Line a large baking tray with baking paper. Roll the mixture into about 2-3 cm (¾-1¼ in) balls and space them evenly on the tray. Bake in the oven for 25 minutes.

Combine the sauce ingredients in a non-stick frying pan and simmer gently for a few minutes before adding the cooked mushroom 'neat-balls'. Continue to simmer for a further few minutes.

To make the pasta, bring a pot of water to the boil. Add the pasta. Reduce the heat and simmer for about 6 minutes before straining.

Serve the mushroom neat-balls and sauce over the fettuccine and top off with a generous sprinkling of cashew 'parmesan' and oregano. Enjoy.

PUMPKIN & CHICKPEA CURRY WITH TOASTED COCONUT CAULI RICE

On a chilly winter night, when you crave something nourishing and warm, you will be glad you made this. The colour and flavour of the toasted coconut cauli rice, the creamy and spicy chickpea curry and the scrumptious roast pumpkin (winter squash) are just perfect. Plus, this combination is packed full of anti-inflammatory turmeric, fibre and healthy, whole, plant-based fats to nourish your body.

Serves 2
Prep time: 10 minutes
Cook time: 40 minutes
Difficulty: Medium

PUMPKIN
500 g (1 lb 2 oz) pumpkin (winter squash), sliced
1 tablespoon coconut aminos*
1 pinch salt

TOASTED COCONUT CAULI RICE
80 g (2¾ oz/½ cup) cashew nuts
½ head (about 400 g/14 oz) cauliflower
15 g (½ oz/¼ cup) shredded coconut

CHICKPEA CURRY
1 onion, diced
2 garlic cloves, minced
225 g (8 oz) cherry tomatoes
2 teaspoons ground cumin
2 teaspoons ground turmeric
2 teaspoons garam masala
½ teaspoon chilli flakes
250 g (9 oz) canned chickpeas, drained and rinsed
250 ml (8½ fl oz/1 cup) coconut milk
¼ teaspoon salt
juice of 1 lemon
15 g (½ oz/½ cup) coriander (cilantro) leaves, plus extra to serve
45 g (1½ oz/1 cup) English spinach

Preheat the oven to 180°C (350°F) fan-forced. Lay the pumpkin out on a baking paper-lined tray, sprinkle with the coconut aminos and salt and place in the oven for 40 minutes while you prepare the rest of the dish.

Pulse the cashew nuts and cauliflower florets in a food processor until you get a rice-like consistency. Add the coconut and stir it through. Spread the mixture on a second baking paper-lined tray and place in the oven. Stir after 10 minutes, then return to the oven for a further 10 minutes.

For the curry, add the onion, garlic, tomatoes and spices to a food processor. Blend until a liquid is formed.

Heat a non-stick frying pan on low. Add the onion and tomato mixture and stir well. Leave to simmer for about 5 minutes. Add the chickpeas and coconut milk. Simmer until the liquid reduces again. Add the salt and the lemon juice. Turn the heat off and stir in the fresh coriander and English spinach.

Divide the pumpkin, toasted cauli rice and curry between two plates and enjoy.

PERFECT
PESTO PASTA

Pesto pasta is one of my all-time favourite meals. Whether it is served for a Sunday night supper, after arriving home from a weekend away, or as a super-quick and tasty weeknight meal. It is always a sure-fire winner. This is the version I most commonly make as I find mung bean fettuccine works an absolute treat. But these days there are so many whole, gluten-free pasta replacements available from your local wholefood store. So far I have tried black bean, mung bean, edamame, brown rice and soy bean pastas. You can also make the pesto ahead of time and freeze it in batches if you have basil growing in abundance.

Serves 2
Prep time: 10 minutes
Cook time: 10 minutes
Difficulty: Easy

PASTA

1 packet (200 g/7 oz) mung bean
  fettuccine*

PESTO

1 cup Cashew 'parmesan' (see page 272)
100 g (3½ oz/2 cups tightly packed) basil
4 tablespoons coconut aminos*
1 teaspoon lemon zest

TO SERVE

2 tablespoons pine nuts, toasted
1 tablespoon basil

Bring a pot of water to the boil. Add the pasta and simmer for 5–10 minutes.

Add the pesto ingredients to a food processor and pulse to combine. If you are in the great outdoors and not using a food processor, finely chop the basil and stir the pesto ingredients together in a bowl.

Once the pasta is cooked, drain and add the pesto mixture. Sprinkle with the toasted pine nuts and basil leaves before serving.

MUSHROOM, LEMON
& THYME RISOTTO

I must confess. Before I started making this zesty and creamy meal I didn't love risotto. I find risottos can sometimes be so salty and rich. I had a go at adding some lemon zest to balance out the 'cheesy' flavour and the result was so tasty and the roast pumpkin (winter squash) balances it perfectly. It is a warming, simple and humble meal to nourish your body and mind. I have used roasted pumpkin in this recipe but you could replace it with sweet potato or roasted tomatoes, whatever is in season, to maximise the flavour.

Serves 2
Prep time: 5 minutes
Cook time: 30 minutes
Difficulty: Medium

RISOTTO

220 g (8 oz) pumpkin (winter squash), peeled and diced

1 onion, thinly sliced

4 garlic cloves, minced

1 litre (34 fl oz/4 cups) vegetable stock

220 g (8 oz/1 cup) short-grain brown rice

zest and juice of 1 lemon

2 tablespoons thyme

270 g (9½ oz) mushrooms, sliced

TO SERVE

1 tablespoon pine nuts

2 tablespoons Cashew 'parmesan' (see page 272)

1 tablespoon thyme

Preheat the oven to 180°C (350°F) fan-forced.

Spread the pumpkin on a baking paper-lined tray and bake in the oven for 30 minutes.

Add the onion, garlic and a dash of vegetable stock to a large saucepan over medium heat. Lightly fry until translucent. Add the rice and stir well before adding the remaining vegetable stock. Bring to the boil and reduce to a simmer for about 30 minutes or until all the liquid is absorbed. Add half of each of the lemon juice, zest, thyme and roast pumpkin. Stir well before turning the heat off. Cover to keep warm.

Heat a non-stick frying pan over medium heat and fry the mushrooms in the remaining lemon juice and thyme until browned. Divide the risotto into serving dishes, top with the mushrooms, the rest of the pumpkin and lemon zest, and serve with the pine nuts and cashew 'parmesan', sprinkled with a little thyme.

CREAMY COCONUT POLENTA
& BALSAMIC VEGGIES

Sometimes you just need something that is ready in a jiffy, fills you up and tastes amazing. Arriving back to the camp site after a big hike or a beach adventure is the perfect time for this dish. It is simple, with a delicious balance of sweet and savoury flavours fusing traditional Mexican and Italian staple ingredients. You don't need a whole heap of exotic ingredients and you can always enjoy it as a side dish to complement a salad or pasta. Plus any leftover polenta is absolutely divine toasted for breakfast the next day topped with Comforting baked beans (see page 46) or avocado and sauerkraut.

Serves 2
Prep time: 10 minutes
Cook time: 30 minutes
Difficulty: Easy

BALSAMIC VEGGIES

150 g (5½ oz) mushrooms, sliced

150 g (5½ oz) red capsicums (bell peppers), sliced

100 g (3½ oz) zucchini (courgettes), sliced

60 g (2 oz/½ cup) olives, pitted

45 g (1½ oz/¾ cup tightly packed) basil, chopped

60 ml (2 fl oz/¼ cup) balsamic vinegar

1 teaspoon garlic powder

POLENTA

150 g (5½ oz/1 cup) polenta

250 ml (8½ fl oz/1 cup) coconut milk

500 ml (17 fl oz/2 cups) water

zest and juice of 1 lemon

TO SERVE

1 tablespoon chopped basil

1 tablespoon balsamic vinegar

1 teaspoon lemon zest

Combine the balsamic veggie ingredients in a bowl. Mix well and set aside.

Combine the polenta ingredients in a saucepan. Whisk well to combine. Place over a low heat and cook slowly, stirring every few minutes to avoid clumps.

Add the balsamic veggies to a saucepan and cook on a low heat, stirring occasionally.

Once the polenta is cooked, pour it into a non-stick frying pan. Place over medium heat until toasted and warmed through.

Top the polenta with the balsamic veggies and serve with the extra fresh basil, balsamic and lemon zest.

MUSHROOM & PARSLEY
CREAMY ALFREDO

This pasta dish is the epitome of comfort food. The pasta I use is easy to find at your local health food store. But you could use any pasta variety you like. The secret to making the sauce as creamy as possible is all in the soaking time of the cashew nuts. Up to eight hours in filtered cold water is ideal. But I am a realist. Most of the time you can forget to do food prep and instead decide on a recipe for dinner on the fly. So, a quick option is to pour boiling water over your cashew nuts and let them soak for about ten minutes. This will soften them enough to blend to a creamy liquid. Be sure to rinse them well before processing.

Serves 2
Prep time: 10 minutes (+ soaking time)
Cook time: 20 minutes
Difficulty: Easy

SAUCE
155 g (5½ oz/1 cup) cashew nuts
250 ml (8½ fl oz/1 cup) vegetable stock
1 tablespoon lemon juice
1 teaspoon garlic powder
20 g (¾ oz/⅓ cup) nutritional yeast*
½ teaspoon salt
60 g (2 oz/1 cup) parsley, finely chopped

PASTA
250 g (9 oz) mushrooms, sliced
1 packet (200 g/7 oz) mung bean
   fettuccine*

TO SERVE
1 tablespoon chopped parsley

Boil 500 ml (17 fl oz/2 cups) of water, pour over the cashew nuts and leave to soak while you prepare the rest of the dish.

Heat a large non-stick frying pan over medium heat and sauté the mushrooms until well cooked. Set aside.

Drain and rinse your cashew nuts. Add them to a high-speed blender or food processor. Add all the other sauce ingredients, except the parsley, and blend until smooth and creamy. Add the chopped parsley, stirring well.

Bring a pot of water to the boil. Add the mung bean fettuccine, reduce to a simmer and cook for 5-8 minutes. Drain, transfer to a bowl and stir in the sauce and sautéed mushrooms. Sprinkle with the extra parsley and serve immediately.

ROAST ROOT VEGGIE WRAPS
WITH WHITE BEAN PESTO

When I used to work in an office, I took this wrap in for lunch nearly every day. I used to roast a big batch of root veggies at the beginning of the week. Then I would take a container of roast veg, pesto and fresh salad greens to the office along with a few mountain bread wraps. Keeping the fillings and wraps separate until you are about to eat them is the key to keeping things fresh. I love to toast mine when there is a sandwich press available, but the wraps are equally yummy untoasted. You can also ditch the wrap altogether and enjoy it all in a big bowl of goodness.

Makes 4 wraps
Prep time: 10 minutes
Cook time: 35 minutes
Difficulty: Easy

ROAST ROOT VEGGIES

150 g (5½ oz) beetroot (beets), diced

150 g (5½ oz) sweet potato, diced

1 tablespoon coconut aminos*

¼ teaspoon salt

¼ teaspoon garlic powder

TO SERVE

8 mountain bread wraps

½ cup White bean pesto (see page 262)

20 g (¾ oz/1 cup loosely packed) rocket (arugula)

75 g (2¾ oz) tomatoes, diced

1 avocado, diced

Preheat the oven to 200°C (400°F) fan-forced. Line a baking tray with baking paper.

Spread the beetroot and sweet potato out on the tray, sprinkle with the coconut aminos, salt and garlic powder. Place in the oven to roast for 30 minutes.

Heat a sandwich press or non-stick frying pan on medium heat.

Assemble the wraps by overlapping two pieces of mountain bread and spreading with white bean pesto. Add the roasted veggies along with the rocket, tomato and avocado. Fold the opposite edges over and roll to enclose all the fillings. Place in the sandwich press or press down with a spatula in a non-stick frying pan. Cook on both sides for a few minutes each. Slice in half and serve.

ZUCCHINI & PUMPKIN SLICE

This slice has all the nostalgia and taste of traditional versions, but is made completely of plant-based, wholefood goodness. In this easy recipe eggs and flour are replaced with hearty chickpea flour (which is sometimes called besan flour). The nutritional yeast, which you can find at your local health or wholefood store, gives it a yummy 'cheesy' flavour. I think zucchini (courgette) and pumpkin work well in this slice, but you could add any veggies you like. The more the merrier!

Serves 4
Prep time: 10 minutes
Cook time: 45 minutes
Difficulty: Easy

SLICE

110 g (4 oz/1 cup) chickpea flour (besan)*

60 g (2 oz/1 cup) nutritional yeast*

75 g (2¾ oz/½ cup) tapioca flour

2 teaspoons vegetable stock powder

1 teaspoon baking powder

1 teaspoon garlic powder

1 tablespoon Cashew 'parmesan'
   (see page 272)

85 ml (2¾ fl oz/⅓ cup) water

1 onion, diced

½ red capsicum (bell pepper), finely diced

135 g (5 oz/1 cup) grated zucchini
   (courgette)

155 g (5½ oz) pumpkin (winter squash),
   peeled and finely diced

TO SERVE

1 tablespoon chopped parsley

Cashew 'parmesan' (see page 272)

Preheat the oven to 180°C (350°F) fan-forced.

Line a medium slice tin or casserole dish with baking paper.

Combine all the dry ingredients in a bowl. Add the water and vegetables and mix well.

Pour into a baking paper-lined tray, sprinkle with the cashew 'parmesan' and bake for 45 minutes or until browned.

Remove from the oven and leave to cool for at least 30 minutes before slicing.

Serve with the parsley and cashew 'parmesan'.

MEXI STUFFED
SWEET POTATOES

In this recipe I have used three different varieties of sweet potato: orange, purple and white. The colour of each is where their unique health benefits lie, but all are packed with fibre and complex carbohydrates. You can use any variety of sweet potato available at your local grocer or farmers' market. The Mexican-inspired fillings are a fresh and colourful stuffing for these sweet potatoes and also work really well in tacos.

Serves 4
Prep time: 10 minutes
Cook time: 60 minutes
Difficulty: Easy

SWEET POTATOES

2 kg (4 lb 6 oz) assorted sweet potatoes
 (approximately)
1 corn cob, cooked
1 red capsicum (bell pepper), diced
1 avocado, sliced
15 g (½ oz/½ cup) coriander (cilantro)
 leaves
250 g (9 oz) canned black beans,
 drained and rinsed

TO SERVE

1 teaspoon smoked paprika*
1 cup 'Cheesy' tahini sauce
 (see page 274)
1 lime, halved

Preheat the oven to 180°C (350°F) fan-forced. Line a baking tray with baking paper.

Lightly score the whole sweet potatoes and place them on the tray. Bake in the oven for about 60 minutes or until cooked through. Once done, turn the oven off and leave the potatoes to rest for 10 minutes or so to soften.

Cut the sweet potatoes in half lengthways.

Cut the kernels off the corn cob and top the sweet potatoes with the corn, capsicum, avocado, coriander and black beans. Sprinkle with the smoked paprika and serve with the 'cheesy' tahini sauce and lime halves.

SMOKY BEETROOT &
BLACK BEAN BURGERS

These burgers are for all the beetroot (beet) fans. The patties are just as yummy served as a traditional version between two buns with all the trimmings. They also freeze well and make great leftovers. You can chop them into salads and wraps or enjoy them as a delicious veggie stack with hummus, sauerkraut and a few herbs. I love contrasting their crunchy texture with a creamy avo mash and some crispy Smoky coconut 'bacon' (see page 278), but you could really add anything you like.

Makes about 4 burgers
Prep time: 10 minutes
Cook time: 25 minutes
Difficulty: Medium

PATTIES
100 g (3½ oz/½ cup) quinoa

30 g (1 oz/½ cup) nutritional yeast*

2 teaspoons ground cumin

2 teaspoons smoked paprika*

1 pinch salt

500 g (1 lb 2 oz) canned black beans, drained and rinsed

210 g (7½ oz/1½ cups) beetroot (beets), grated

1 red onion, finely diced

TO SERVE
1 avocado

juice of 1 lime

25 g (1 oz/½ cup) English spinach

1 ripe tomato, sliced

½ cup Quick pickled onion (see page 264)

½ cup Smoky coconut 'bacon' (see page 278)

1 teaspoon sesame seeds

Preheat the oven to 200°C (400°F) fan-forced.

Blitz the dry burger ingredients in a food processor until a coarse flour is formed. Transfer to a bowl and add the black beans, beetroot and onion. Stir and lightly mash until the mixture is well combined and sticking together.

Line a large baking tray with baking paper. Mould the mixture into eight burger patties. Evenly space them out on the baking tray and lightly press them down with a spatula.

Bake in the oven for 20 minutes. Flip the burgers and bake for a further 5 minutes.

Combine the avocado and lime juice and roughly mash.

To assemble your burgers, stack one burger with spinach, tomato, mashed avocado, pickled onion and coconut 'bacon'. Top with a second burger, sprinkle with sesame seeds and serve. Enjoy!

SIMPLE
STIR-FRY

When I have leftover veggies in the fridge this is one of my go-to dishes to use them up. Waste not, want not. And the more variety the better. My hot tip for the perfect stir-fry is to turn the heat off before the veggies start to become too soft. That crunch in the final dish is what you are chasing. To feed a few more hungry mouths, serve with cooked brown rice, quinoa, or the yummy Toasted coconut cauli rice from page 124.

Serves 2
Prep time: 10 minutes
Cook time: 15 minutes
Difficulty: Easy

STIR-FRY

3 garlic cloves, minced

1 tablespoon minced fresh ginger

½ teaspoon chilli powder

½ teaspoon ground turmeric

1 tablespoon miso*

2 tablespoons coconut aminos*

225 g (8 oz) button mushrooms, sliced

1 red capsicum (bell pepper), diced

120 g (4½ oz) broccolini, chopped

55 g (2 oz/¾ cup) red cabbage, shredded

TO SERVE

2 tablespoons almonds, toasted and chopped

2 tablespoons sesame seeds

Heat a non-stick frying pan on medium.

Combine the garlic, ginger, chilli powder, turmeric, miso and coconut aminos in a bowl and whisk together. Add the mushrooms and stir to coat well. Transfer to the frying pan and cook until softened. Add the capsicum and broccolini, stirring well.

When all the vegetables are cooked through, turn the heat off, add the red cabbage and stir once more.

Transfer to serving plates, sprinkle with the chopped almonds and sesame seeds and serve. Yum.

SWEET POTATO, EGGPLANT & 'RICOTTA' LASAGNE

I have been working on perfecting this recipe for years. The challenge? How to create a perfect lasagne that doesn't take hours to make, yet is just as hearty, warming and, most of all, tasty as the traditional versions. The secret is the quality of the ingredients. I always make sure the tofu I buy is organic, which is so readily available these days. When it comes to the veggies, in-season will always have more flavour. You could try thinly sliced zucchini (courgettes), pumpkin (winter squash), squash or mushrooms.

Serves 4
Prep time: 30 minutes
Cook time: 1½ hours
Difficulty: Easy

400 g (14 oz) canned diced tomatoes
2 garlic cloves, minced
300 g (10½ oz) firm tofu*, mashed
2 tablespoons miso*
20 g (¾ oz/⅓ cup) nutritional yeast*
juice of 1 lemon
1 teaspoon freshly ground black pepper
30 g (1 oz/1 cup, loosely packed) basil, finely chopped
1 small eggplant (aubergine), thinly sliced
1 small sweet potato, thinly sliced
¼ cup Cashew 'parmesan' (see page 272)

Preheat the oven to 180°C (350°F) fan-forced.

Combine the tomatoes and garlic in a small saucepan and bring to the boil. Reduce to a simmer, stirring occasionally, until the mixture thickens. Set aside.

In a mixing bowl, combine the tofu, miso, nutritional yeast, lemon juice, black pepper and basil. Mix well.

Spread half the tomato mixture over the base of a casserole dish. Add a layer of sliced eggplant followed by a layer of the tofu mixture, followed by a layer of sliced sweet potato. Repeat this process making the final layer a generous sprinkling of cashew 'parmesan'.

Cover with foil and place in the oven to bake for 40 minutes. Uncover and return to the oven for a further 30–40 minutes. Enjoy!

RAINBOW
CAULI FRIED RICE

Finely chopped or grated cauliflower has the most amazing rice-like texture, making it a nifty way to sneak more veg onto your plate. This is one of my favourite ways to enjoy it – as a classic fried rice. I like to combine mine with loads of colourful, crunchy veggies and a generous splash of fermented coconut aminos for extra flavour. It is such a nourishing way to shake up regular old fried rice.

Serves 2
Prep time: 10 minutes
Cook time: 20 minutes
Difficulty: Medium

CAULI RICE

½ head (400 g/14 oz) cauliflower

155 g (5½ oz/1 cup) cashew nuts

1 onion, diced

2 garlic cloves, minced

80 g (2¾ oz) edamame, or peas

½ red capsicum (bell pepper), diced

30 g (1 oz/½ cup) spring onions
   (scallions), sliced

2 tablespoons tamari*

TO SERVE

45 g (1½ oz/½ cup) red cabbage,
   shredded

7 g (¼ oz/¼ cup) coriander (cilantro)
   leaves

1 tablespoon coconut aminos*

Break the cauliflower into florets and add to a food processor with the cashew nuts. Pulse to combine. Once a rice-like texture is achieved, set aside.

Heat a non-stick frying pan over low heat. Sauté the onion and garlic until translucent.

Add the cauliflower mixture to the frying pan with the edamame, capsicum and spring onion and continue to cook for a few minutes. Add the tamari and stir well. Continue to cook, stirring often, for about 10 minutes.

Once cooked, turn the heat off and add the shredded cabbage and coriander, stirring well. Drizzle the coconut aminos all over just before serving.

CURRIED
ROAST VEGGIE SOUP

Where we live, even autumn and spring can be a bit brisk. A good, hearty soup is the perfect antidote to these cooler days. Enter my favourite soup recipe ever. It is bursting with flavour and colour. Veggies, coconut and spices were just made to be together and lend themselves perfectly to this soup. It is so thick that you can make it go further by serving it over brown rice and topping it with some coconut yoghurt and coriander (cilantro) like a curry.

Serves 4
Prep time: 10 minutes
Cook time: 50 minutes
Difficulty: Medium

ROAST VEGGIES

1 kg (2 lb 3 oz) butternut pumpkin
   (squash), peeled and diced,
   seeds saved
2 tablespoons coconut aminos*
1 red capsicum (bell pepper), diced
1 zucchini (courgette), diced
3 carrots, diced
2 teaspoons curry powder
2 teaspoons garlic powder
2 teaspoons smoked paprika*

SOUP

2 onions, peeled and diced
2 tablespoons coconut aminos*
400 ml (13½ fl oz) coconut milk
250 ml (8½ fl oz/1 cup) vegetable stock
2 teaspoons ground turmeric

TO SERVE

1 tablespoon sliced fresh chilli
1 tablespoon sliced spring onion
   (scallions)

Preheat the oven to 200°C (400°F) fan-forced.

Rinse the pumpkin seeds, pat them dry and toss in half of the coconut aminos. Place on a baking tray in the oven for 10 minutes while you prepare the rest of the dish.

Combine the capsicum, zucchini and carrot on two large baking paper-lined trays. Coat in the remaining coconut aminos and the spices.

Place in the oven to roast for 30 minutes.

Meanwhile, heat a large saucepan over medium heat. Sauté the onion in the coconut aminos until translucent. Add the coconut milk, vegetable stock and turmeric. Stir well and simmer until fragrant. Add the roast veggies. Bring to the boil and simmer for a few more minutes.

Turn the heat off and, using a hand-held blender, blend until smooth and creamy.

Top with the roasted pumpkin seeds, sliced red chilli and sliced spring onion.

'CHEESY' ZUCCHINI NOODLE BAKE

You really can't get a simpler recipe than this, but it still packs in the veggies, flavour and quality plant-based fats. It's nutrient-dense, warming and has a divine 'cheesy' flavour. The parsley is such a sneaky nourishing ingredient as it is super high in vitamins and minerals and a little goes a long way with flavour. I like making this with zucchini (courgette) noodles, but you could also cook your choice of pasta and use that instead.

Serves 2
Prep time: 5 minutes
Cook time: 40 minutes
Difficulty: Very easy

400 g (14 oz) zucchini (courgettes),
   spiralised
30 g (1 oz/½ cup) spring onions
   (scallions), thinly sliced
60 g (2 oz/1 cup) parsley, finely chopped
1 cup Cashew 'parmesan' (see page 272)

Preheat the oven to 180°C (350°F) fan-forced.

In a large mixing bowl, combine all the ingredients, saving about ¼ cup of the cashew 'parmesan'. Mix well.

Line a small casserole dish with baking paper and transfer the mixture into it.

Sprinkle all of the remaining 'parmesan' over the top and place in the oven to bake for about 40 minutes.

SHARE

EGGPLANT
VEGGIE PATCH PIZZAS

Roasting these mini pizzas, made entirely of veggies, brings out the flavour of the eggplant (aubergine). You may think a pizza isn't a pizza without cheese, but trust me and try the Cashew 'parmesan' (see page 272) – I think it's a perfect topping for pizza. I love to make these in late summer and early autumn when some of the ingredients are abundant in our veggie patch.

Makes about 12 mini pizzas
Prep time: 10 minutes
Cook time: 30 minutes
Difficulty: Easy

PIZZAS

500 g (1 lb 2 oz) eggplant (aubergine),
   sliced into rounds, 1 cm (½ in) thick
125 ml (4 fl oz/½ cup) tomato paste
¼ red onion, diced
½ red capsicum (bell pepper), diced
75 g (2¾ oz) button mushrooms, sliced
15 g (½ oz/½ cup loosely packed) basil
90 g (3 oz/¾ cup) black olives, pitted

TO SERVE

1 tablespoon Cashew 'parmesan'
   (see page 272)
basil

Preheat the oven to 180°C (350°F) fan-forced.

Line a large baking tray with baking paper and evenly space the eggplant slices on the tray. Place in the oven to bake for 10 minutes.

Remove from the oven, spread the slices with tomato paste and add all the other toppings.

Return to the oven to bake for another 20 minutes.

Sprinkle with the cashew 'parmesan' and extra basil before serving.

'RICOTTA' BRUSCHETTA
ON TOASTED OATY SEED LOAF

Brushchetta is one of those beautifully simple yet flavourful Italian inventions I can't get enough of. I have shaken up the classic version and added a very easy-to-make tofu 'ricotta'. It combines protein and amino acid-rich tofu with probiotic miso and B vitamin-packed nutritional yeast. The result is oh-so satisfying. It's perfect for a picnic or a light meal at the end of a warm day.

Makes 6 pieces
Prep time: 15 minutes
Cook time: 5 minutes
Difficulty: Easy

BRUSCHETTA

160 g (5½ oz) cherry tomatoes, finely diced

½ red capsicum (bell pepper), finely diced

⅓ small red onion, finely diced

15 g (½ oz/½ cup loosely packed) basil, finely chopped

60 g (2 oz/½ cup) olives, pitted and finely diced

1 tablespoon balsamic vinegar

6 slices Oaty seed loaf (see page 254)

'RICOTTA'

1 teaspoon onion powder

1 teaspoon garlic powder

2 tablespoons miso*

juice of 1 lemon

1 tablespoon nutritional yeast*

2 tablespoons water

300 g (10½ oz) organic silken tofu*

Combine the tomatoes, capsicum, red onion, basil, olives and balsamic vinegar in a bowl. Mix well.

Combine all the 'ricotta' ingredients, except for the tofu, in a bowl. Whisk until smooth.

Drain the tofu and pat dry with paper towel. Roughly mash it with a fork, add the 'ricotta' mixture and gently fold until evenly combined. Set aside.

Toast the bread slices, spread with a generous amount of 'ricotta' and top with the bruschetta mixture.

Enjoy immediately.

SPINACH & OLIVE
SPANAKOPITA

So you think you can't create a plant-based version of spanakopita? Give this one a try. It is amazing what a little tofu, miso and nutritional yeast can do to create the 'cheesy' texture and flavour of ricotta. I have added olives to this recipe to give it a salty flavour and really bring the filling to life. I have found that mountain bread wraps, available at your local wholefood store or supermarket, are a perfect substitute for refined pastry. But if you are after a gluten-free alternative, a gluten-free wrap will do the trick.

Makes 16 pieces
Prep time: 15 minutes
Cook time: 30 minutes
Difficulty: Medium

1 onion, diced

3 garlic cloves, minced

135 g (5 oz/3 cups) English spinach, chopped

250 g (9 oz) firm tofu*, drained and crumbled

60 g (2 oz/½ cup) olives, diced

1 tablespoon miso*

3 tablespoons nutritional yeast*

zest and juice of 1 lemon

8 mountain bread wraps

1 tablespoon coconut aminos*

1 tablespoon sesame seeds

Preheat the oven to 180°C (350°F) fan-forced.

Sauté the onion and garlic in a saucepan until soft and translucent. Add the spinach, tofu, olives, miso, nutritional yeast, lemon zest and juice. Stir well and continue to cook until all the liquid is absorbed.

Cut the mountain bread wraps in half lengthways. Spoon 1 tablespoon of the cooked mixture onto one end of each strip and form into triangles by folding on the diagonal a number of times. Brush a little coconut aminos on the end and fold up.

Lay out on a baking paper-lined tray. Brush with coconut aminos and sprinkle with sesame seeds.

Bake for 15 minutes or until golden brown and crispy. Enjoy!

SPICED CHICKPEA
FLATBREADS

Spiced chickpeas are an absolute staple of mine and this is one of my favourite ways to enjoy them. I think it is a perfect dish to share and also makes a great easy dinner when you are pushed for time. The quinoa bases are incredibly filling and hearty, not to mention gluten-free. If you are all out of quinoa or need a lighter base, you can replace these bases with a whole grain wrap.

Makes 2 flatbreads
Prep time: 10 minutes
Cook time: 20 minutes
Difficulty: Easy

BASES
150 g (5½ oz/¾ cup) white quinoa
½ teaspoon baking powder

TOPPINGS
1 tablespoon pine nuts
1 cup Miso hummus (see page 266)
1½ cups Spiced chickpeas (see page 270)
2 tablespoons roughly chopped flat-leaf
   (Italian) parsley

Preheat the oven to 180°C (350°F) fan-forced.

To make the bases, line two large baking trays with baking paper. Rinse the quinoa well under running water. Add to a blender or food processor with 375 ml (12½ fl oz/ 1½ cups) of water and the baking powder. Process on high speed until super smooth. Spread the mixture out on the prepared trays and bake in the oven for 20 minutes.

Heat a frying pan over low heat and lightly toast the pine nuts.

To serve, spread the hummus over both flatbreads. Scatter with the spiced chickpeas, parsley and toasted pine nuts. Slice into quarters and serve.

SWEET POTATO NACHOS

This recipe for wholefood nachos could not be further from the 'packet of corn chips, jar of salsa, packet of cheese' version. I love taking classics and re-creating them out of whole veggies. The challenge, though, is to achieve a great flavour that reminds you of the original and yet holds its own. These sweet potato nachos are so yummy. They will leave you feeling completely satisfied, nourished and full of energy.

Serves 2
Prep time: 15 minutes
Cook time: 30 minutes
Difficulty: Easy

SWEET POTATO CHIPS

1 kg (2 lb 3 oz) sweet potato
juice of 1 lime
1 teaspoon smoked paprika*
¼ teaspoon salt

TOPPINGS

1 corn cob
250 g (9 oz) canned black beans, drained and rinsed
1½ cups Fresh salsa (see page 268)
1 avocado, sliced
1 cup 'Cheesy' tahini sauce (see page 274)
1 lime, quartered

Preheat the oven to 200°C (400°F) fan-forced.

Line a large baking tray with baking paper. Slice the sweet potato into thin wedge shapes and spread out on the tray. Sprinkle with the lime juice, paprika and salt. Cook for about 30 minutes.

Cut the kernels from the cob. Heat a non-stick frying pan over medium heat and lightly char the corn kernels.

Once cooked, layer the sweet potato chips and top with the corn, black beans, salsa and avocado. Sprinkle with the 'cheesy' tahini sauce and serve with a few lime wedges. Enjoy.

LEMON PEPPER
'CHEESY BREADS'

There has been a Christmas tradition in my family from before I can remember. We call it 'cheesy bread'. The traditional version is made of pita bread, butter, parmesan and lemon pepper. Having discovered a way to make parmesan out of cashew nuts, I saw the opportunity to turn this nostalgic favourite upside down. It worked! It brings back all the happy memories minus the dairy. For a gluten-free version you can substitute the mountain bread for thin, gluten-free wraps.

Makes 4 large pieces
Prep time: 5 minutes
Cook time: 10 minutes
Difficulty: Very easy

4 mountain bread wraps

2 tablespoons coconut aminos*

½ cup Cashew 'parmesan' (see page 272)

juice of 1 lemon

1 teaspoon freshly ground black pepper

Preheat the oven to 180°C (350°F) fan-forced.

Line two large baking trays with baking paper. Evenly brush one side of each wrap with coconut aminos. Sprinkle with the cashew 'parmesan', lemon juice and pepper.

Bake for 10–15 minutes or until the toppings begin to brown. Remove from the oven and leave to cool until crispy.

Serve as is or break up into smaller, chip-sized pieces. Enjoy as an addition to a platter with dips or on its own.

SUPER GREEN SUMMER ROLLS
WITH TANGY MISO SAUCE

The crisp crunch of these super green summer rolls is so satisfying. They make a great appetiser to a summer meal for friends – or keep a batch all to yourself. Either way, they are delicious and the miso sauce will have you licking the bowl. Plus, they are a great way to pack more greens into your meal. Greens such as English spinach are high in calcium, magnesium, zinc and protein.

Makes about 10 rolls
Prep time: 30 minutes
Difficulty: Easy

SUMMER ROLLS
1 lemon
1 avocado, sliced
10 rice paper sheets
90 g (3 oz/2 cups) English spinach
1 small cucumber, ribboned
25 g (1 oz/½ cup) coriander (cilantro) leaves
1 tablespoon sesame seeds

TO SERVE
½ cup Tangy miso sauce (see page 276)

Squeeze the lemon over the sliced avocado to preserve its freshness.

Carefully fill a large, deep bowl with hot but not boiling water. Slide a rice paper sheet into the bowl of water and gently submerge. Wait 2 minutes until the rice paper becomes translucent before removing it and placing on a flat, smooth surface.

Immediately place another sheet of rice paper into the plate of water.

Fill your prepared rice paper sheet with a little of all the summer roll ingredients and gently roll it up, folding the sides in as you go. Repeat this process for the remainder.

Serve with the tangy miso sauce.

FRESH
TOSTADITAS

It's no secret I love Mexican flavours. They are fresh, healthy and tasty. These tostaditas make the most perfect picnic fodder or simple snack. The creamy avocado combined with fresh salsa and crunchy tortilla chips is heavenly. If you are taking them on a picnic or to enjoy elsewhere, store the components separately and assemble on location to preserve that perfect crisp crunch. Stock up on good-quality corn tortillas at an international food store or a wholefoods store. When toasted in the oven they make a great alternative to processed corn chips.

Makes about 24 pieces
Prep time: 5 minutes
Cook time: 15 minutes
Difficulty: Very easy

CORN TORTILLA CHIPS
8 small corn tortillas
juice of 1 lime
¼ teaspoon salt

TOPPING
2 avocados
juice of 1 lime
¼ teaspoon salt
½ teaspoon freshly ground black pepper
1½ cups Fresh salsa (see page 268)

TO SERVE
1 tablespoon chopped coriander
   (cilantro) leaves
1 tablespoon coconut aminos*

Preheat the oven to 200°C (400°F) fan-forced.

Line two large baking trays with baking paper. Cut the corn tortillas into quarters. Lay them on the tray. Sprinkle with the lime juice and salt. Place in the oven to bake for 15 minutes.

In a small bowl, mash the avocados. Stir in the remaining lime juice, the salt and the pepper.

Once the tortilla quarters are baked, remove them from the oven and spread them out on a serving platter. Top each with the avocado mixture and salsa. Sprinkle with a little extra coriander and coconut aminos and serve.

ZUCCHINI &
SWEET CORN FRITTERS

I think these fritters are best enjoyed warm, but they freeze and thaw well and reheat easily in a sandwich press with a sprinkling of water. A batch of them makes a great addition to a dinner table spread with a few other share options. They are full of goodies like legumes, veggies and herbs, as well as fresh tangy flavours from the salsa.

Makes about 12 fritters
Prep time: 5 minutes
Cook time: 20 minutes
Difficulty: Easy

FRITTERS
125 g (4½ oz) chickpea flour (besan)*

15 g (½ oz/¼ cup) nutritional yeast*

1 teaspoon garlic powder

1 teaspoon baking powder

½ teaspoon salt

200 g (7 oz/1½ cups) zucchini
  (courgettes), grated

400 g (14 oz/2 cups) corn kernels

1 onion, finely diced

15 g (½ oz/½ cup) flat-leaf (Italian)
  parsley, finely chopped

125 g (4½ oz/½ cup) coconut yoghurt*

TO SERVE
1½ cups Fresh salsa (see page 268)

Heat a non-stick frying pan on low.

Mix all the dry ingredients together. Add the rest of the fritter ingredients and mix well.

Mould into small portions and flatten them down in the frying pan with a spatula. Cook for 5-10 minutes on each side.

Serve with a side of fresh salsa.

SPICY WEDGES &
SWEET CHILLI AÏOLI

Crisp spicy potatoes, fresh lime and creamy sweet chilli aïoli is a winning combination. I like to make these scrumptious wedges for friends and family and they're always hugely popular. Potatoes are a nutritious choice, loaded with vitamin C, fibre and more potassium than a banana.

Serves 2
Prep time: 5 minutes
Cook time: 40 minutes
Difficulty: Very easy

WEDGES

1 kg (2 lb 3 oz) red-skinned potatoes, washed
2 tablespoons coconut aminos*
juice of ½ lemon
1 teaspoon garlic powder
½ teaspoon chilli powder
2 teaspoons smoked paprika*
½ teaspoon cayenne pepper

TO SERVE

1 lime, quartered
½ cup Sweet chilli aïoli (see page 258)

Preheat the oven to 180°C (350°F) fan-forced.

Cut the potatoes into wedges.

Combine all the wedge ingredients, except the potatoes, in a large mixing bowl and whisk to combine. Add the potatoes and toss until well coated.

Line a baking tray with baking paper and space the wedges out on the tray. Place in the oven for 20 minutes. Turn each potato and return to the oven for a further 20-30 minutes or until crisp and golden.

Once the wedges are cooked serve with a squeeze of lime, and the sweet chilli aïoli as a dip.

FIG, ROCKET & 'NOTZZARELLA' PESTO PIZZA

I love to create colourful pizzas from what we have available in the garden, or keep it minimal and top with a simple combination of tomato sauce, mushrooms and fresh basil. We tend to enjoy this fig and pesto combination more when figs are in season. But there are so many winter veggie substitutes you can use to create a great seasonal pizza in the cooler months. In winter I like to roast a big batch of root veggies with rosemary, swap out the basil in the pesto for kale and add some yummy olives.

Makes 2 small pizzas
Prep time: 20 minutes
Cook time: 30 minutes
Difficulty: Easy

BASE

100 g (3½ oz/½ cup) white quinoa
½ teaspoon baking powder

PESTO

½ cup Cashew 'parmesan' (see page 272)
50 g (1¾ oz/1 cup tightly packed) basil
2 tablespoons coconut aminos*
½ teaspoon lemon zest

TOPPINGS

½ cup 'Cashew notzzarella' (see page 260)
2 ripe figs, sliced
1 tablespoon pine nuts
20 g (¾ oz/1 cup loosely packed) rocket (arugula)
1 tablespoon balsamic vinegar

Preheat the oven to 180°C (350°F) fan-forced.

To make the bases, line two large baking trays with baking paper. Rinse the quinoa well under running water and add to a blender or food processor with the baking powder and 250 ml (8½ fl oz/1 cup) water. Process on high-speed until super smooth. Pour out over the two trays and place in the oven for 20 minutes.

Meanwhile, combine the pesto ingredients in a food processor and pulse to combine. Spread evenly over the bases and top with the 'notzzarella', sliced figs and pine nuts. Place in the oven for 10 minutes. Remove and sprinkle with the fresh rocket and a drizzle of balsamic vinegar. Slice, serve and enjoy!

PUMPKIN & BROWN RICE ARANCINI

If you have leftover brown rice, this is a perfect way to use it. You get to avoid waste as well as make something tasty. It's also a good recipe to make a big batch of on a Sunday for your weekly food prep. These arancini travel so well and you can add them to a lunchbox of greens and roasted veggies. I also like to add them to platters or crumble them and toast them in a tasty wrap. The options are endless.

Makes about 16 balls
Prep time: 20 minutes
Cook time: 30 minutes
Difficulty: Easy

140 g (5 oz/¾ cup) long-grain brown rice, rinsed and drained

300 g (10½ oz) pumpkin (winter squash), peeled and diced

1 cup Cashew 'parmesan' (see page 272)

25 g (1 oz/½ cup) chives, chopped

Preheat the oven to 180°C (350°F) fan-forced and line a baking tray with baking paper.

Bring the rice and 500 ml (17 fl oz/2 cups) of water to the boil and reduce to a simmer until all the water is absorbed.

Steam the pumpkin until soft. Combine the steamed pumpkin, cooked brown rice, 'parmesan' and chives in a mixing bowl and stir well to combine.

Line a baking tray with baking paper. Mould the mixture into balls and evenly space them out on the tray. Place in the oven to cook for 30 minutes.

RAW RAINBOW SUSHI WITH QUICK PICKLED GINGER

This recipe is based on traditional sushi but it doesn't have many of the same ingredients. I've kept the main one, the nori, which is traditionally made by shredding and rack-drying seaweed. Organic nori wraps hold impressive amounts of nutrients including iodine. All of that nutritious seaweed wrapped over colourful crunchy veg and cauliflower rice certainly makes for a nourishing meal or snack.

Makes about 6 hand rolls
Prep time: 30 minutes
Difficulty: Medium

SUSHI

1 head (500 g/1 lb 2 oz) cauliflower, broken into florets

310 g (11 oz/2 cups) cashew nuts

1 tablespoon sesame seeds

6 sheets organic nori*

20 g (¾ oz/½ cup) pea shoots, chopped

1 small beetroot (beet), peeled and grated

1 red capsicum (bell pepper), thinly sliced

1 carrot, grated

1 avocado, sliced

TO SERVE

2 tablespoons coconut aminos*

Quick pickled ginger (see page 56)

pea shoots

Add the cauliflower, cashew nuts and sesame seeds to a food processor and pulse until a rice-like texture is achieved.

Place a nori sheet on a bamboo rolling mat. Spoon on a generous amount of the rice mixture and spread it three-quarters of the way across the nori sheet beginning 2 cm (¾ in) from the end. Layer with the raw veggies.

Carefully roll your sushi two-thirds of the way and gently squeeze. Lightly brush the opposite side with some water before rolling all the way and gently pushing closed.

Repeat this process until all the ingredients are used.

Slice with a wet sharp knife, garnish with pea shoots and serve with the coconut aminos, quick pickled ginger and, if you like, sesame seeds.

EPIC SHARE PLATTER

This is such a colourful and abundant platter of goodness. It is well worth going to the extra effort to prepare your toasted tortilla chips, roasted pumpkin, arancini, spiced chickpeas, super green summer rolls and hummus. It feeds quite a few hungry mouths and is such a lovely social, slow way to enjoy food. I like to cook the roast pumpkin ahead of time because it softens after it is cooked and becomes a sweet and savoury spread to go with the tangy fermented veggies and creamy avocado. This platter is so full of variety and taste that even the most avid cheese lover will not notice its absence.

Serves about 8
Prep time: 10 minutes (+ pre-preparation)
Difficulty: Medium

2 cups tortilla chips (see page 172)

1 batch roasted pumpkin (see page 76)

1 batch Pumpkin and brown rice arancini
   (see page 180)

1 cup Spiced chickpeas (see page 270)

5 Super green summer rolls
   (see page 170)

1 cup Miso hummus (see page 266)

125 g (4½ oz/1 cup) black olives, pitted

85 g (3 oz) gherkins

40 g (1½ oz) artichokes in brine, drained

50 g (1¾ oz) fresh cucumber, sliced

50 g (1¾ oz) red capsicum (bell pepper),
   sliced

seeds of ½ pomegranate

250 g (9 oz/1 cup) sauerkraut*

1 avocado, halved lengthways

1 tablespoon sesame seeds

7 g (¼ oz/¼ cup) basil, to serve

Prepare your summer rolls and hummus.

To serve, assemble all the components on a platter and sprinkle the avocado halves with sesames seeds. Scatter the basil leaves over the platter and serve.

MEZZE
PLATTER

A mezze platter is traditionally a selection of small dishes to accompany drinks. The spread can consist of many different items. I love combining a selection of easy-to-prepare dips and home-made crispbreads, such as the 'cheesy breads' from page 168, with a generous amount of crunchy fresh veggies to give variety, texture and fresh flavour. For this version I have included a very simple pared-back tabouleh with my favourite basic hummus and an easy minty tzatziki. A perfect combo to enjoy with friends.

Serves about 4
Prep time: 20 minutes (+ pre-preparation)
Difficulty: Easy

TABOULEH

15 g (½ oz/½ cup) flat-leaf (Italian)
   parsley, finely chopped
1 tablespoon finely diced red onion
½ red capsicum (bell pepper), finely diced
1 teaspoon lemon juice

MINTY TZATZIKI

125 g (4½ oz/½ cup) coconut yoghurt*
1 tablespoon chopped mint
1 teaspoon maple syrup*
1 teaspoon garlic powder
1 teaspoon lemon juice

TO SERVE

1 batch Lemon pepper 'cheesy breads'
   (see page 168)
½ cup Miso hummus (see page 266)
70 g (2½ oz) Quick pickled onion (see
   page 264)
80 g (2¾ oz) cherry tomatoes
60 g (2 oz/½ cup) olives, pitted
50 g (1¾ oz) radishes
80 g (2¾ oz) artichokes in brine, drained

Combine the tabouleh ingredients in a bowl and mix well.

Add the minty tzatziki ingredients to a small bowl and mix to combine.

Assemble everything on a platter and serve.

SWEET

NUT-FREE PROBIOTIC
CHOC MINT 'ICE CREAM' CAKE

Nut-free, gluten-free, grain-free, wholefood and probiotic - this cake is such a winner. It is light yet creamy, crunchy yet also smooth. Easy to make and it keeps really well in the freezer. Plus, it is made from ingredients that are easy to source these days. I get the activated buckwheat and the food-grade peppermint essential oil from my local health food store. If you don't have coconut yoghurt on hand, a thick, canned coconut milk will also do the trick.

Serves about 12
Prep time: 30 minutes (+ freezing time)
Cook time: 10 minutes
Difficulty: Medium

ICE CREAM
600 g (1 lb 5 oz) sweet potato, peeled and diced
185 g (6½ oz/¾ cup) coconut yoghurt*
45 g (1½ oz/⅓ cup) cacao powder*
85 ml (2¾ fl oz/⅓ cup) maple syrup*
1 teaspoon vanilla powder*

BASE
170 g (6 oz/1 cup) activated buckwheat*
90 g (3 oz/1 cup) desiccated coconut
10 medjool dates*, pitted
1 pinch salt

TO SERVE
1 tablespoon cacao nibs*
1 tablespoon mint leaves

Steam the sweet potato and add it to a food processor with the other ice cream ingredients. Pulse to combine and blend until smooth. Line a small cake or slice tin with baking paper and add the ice cream mixture. Place in the freezer for a minimum of 4 hours to set.

Place all the base ingredients in a food processor. Pulse to combine, then process on high speed until the mixture begins to stick together.

Evenly press into a springform cake tin and place in the freezer to set.

Remove the ice cream from the freezer and break it into small pieces. Add to the food processor again, pulse to break up and blend for a short time until a smooth consistency is achieved, taking care not to heat the mixture.

Spread the ice cream over the cake base and return to the freezer. When you are ready to serve, remove the cake from the tin and let sit for 5-10 minutes before cutting. Decorate with the cacao nibs and mint leaves.

CARROT CAKE WITH BLUEBERRY 'CREAM CHEESE' FROSTING

I think this is the ultimate celebration cake. The flavour and texture of both the filling and the frosting is ridiculously close to that of a traditional version laden with butter, sugar and flour. If you are not keen on going to the effort of making a few layers, you can also just use one larger cake tin for the whole thing and cut the process in half. It depends if you are creating it for a special occasion or just to devour in a few bites.

Serves 12 or more
Prep time: 30 minutes (+ setting time)
Cook time: 10 minutes
Difficulty: Medium

FILLING
440 g (15½ oz) carrot, grated
200 g (7 oz/2 cups) walnuts
120 g (4½ oz/2 cups) shredded coconut
10 medjool dates*, pitted
2 teaspoons ground ginger
2 teaspoons ground cinnamon
½ teaspoon ground nutmeg

FROSTING
390 g (14 oz/2½ cups) cashew nuts
125 g (4½ oz/½ cup) coconut yoghurt*
zest and juice of 2 lemons
2 teaspoons miso*
125 ml (4 fl oz/½ cup) maple syrup*
1 tablespoon nutritional yeast*
¼ teaspoon vanilla powder*

TO SERVE
150 g (5½ oz/1 cup) fresh or frozen blueberries
1 tablespoon dried edible flowers
1 tablespoon crushed pistachio nuts

Preheat the oven to 180°C (350°F) fan-forced and place the blueberries on a baking paper-lined tray. Bake for about 10 minutes. Set aside.

Boil 750 ml (25½ fl oz/3 cups) of water and pour over the cashew nuts. Leave to soak while you prepare the filling.

Add all the filling ingredients to a food processor and pulse until you get a cake-like texture. Divide the mixture between three 18 cm (7 in) springform cake tins and gently press down all the way to the edges. Place in the freezer while you prepare the frosting.

Drain and rinse the cashew nuts. Add to a blender with all the other frosting ingredients. Pulse to combine and blend until smooth and creamy. Remove two of the cake tins from the freezer and divide half of the frosting over them, spreading it evenly over both. Return to the freezer, place the rest of the frosting in the fridge and leave to set for 1 hour minimum.

Gently remove all the layers from the tins and layer one over the other, finishing with the one not yet frosted. Cover the entire cake with the remainder of the frosting and scatter with the baked blueberries, dried edible flowers and pistachio nuts. Allow to thaw for 10 minutes before cutting (longer if frozen for a longer period). Store in the freezer.

SWEET POTATO PROBIOTIC 'ICE CREAM' THREE WAYS

Sweet potato ice cream. Who would have thought? You may have noticed I think sweet potatoes are pretty amazing veggies. They are so versatile, filling – and did I mention healthy? One of the ways I like to enjoy them is in this yummy, light and creamy probiotic ice cream, which is surprisingly easy to make. There is also a bit of magic to this ice cream. Instead of melting into a puddle, as it thaws it holds its shape and turns into a beautiful mousse. So no hurrying through your serve. You can savour it slowly.

Makes about 4 scoops
Prep time: 20 minutes (+ setting time)
Difficulty: Easy

AFTER-DINNER MINT

450 g (1 lb) sweet potato, peeled and
   diced
60 g (2 oz/¼ cup) coconut yoghurt*
60 ml (2 fl oz/¼ cup) maple syrup*
45 g (1½ oz/⅓ cup) cacao powder*
1 teaspoon vanilla powder*
1 pinch salt
1 drop food-grade peppermint
   essential oil*

TO SERVE
2 mint sprigs
1 teaspoon cacao nibs*
1 teaspoon crushed pistachio nuts

BEETROOT, RASPBERRY & LIME

300 g (10½ oz) sweet potato, peeled
   and diced
150 g (5½ oz) beetroot (beets), peeled
   and diced
75 g (2¾ oz/½ cup) fresh or frozen
   raspberries
zest and juice of ½ lime
60 g (2 oz/¼ cup) coconut yoghurt*
60 ml (2 fl oz/¼ cup) maple syrup*
1 teaspoon vanilla powder*
1 pinch salt

TO SERVE
1 tablespoon fresh, frozen or dried berries
1 teaspoon dried edible flowers

→

CHOCOLATE
ORANGE

---

450 g (1 lb) sweet potato, peeled and
  diced
60 g (2 oz/¼ cup) coconut yoghurt*
60 ml (2 fl oz/¼ cup) maple syrup*
45 g (1½ oz/⅓ cup) cacao powder*
1 teaspoon vanilla powder*
1 pinch salt
juice of 1 orange
4 drops food-grade orange essential oil*

TO SERVE
2 teaspoons orange zest
1 teaspoon cacao nibs*

Line a metal slice tin with baking paper and place in the freezer.

Steam the sweet potato (and beetroot) until soft. Combine the steamed sweet potato (and beetroot) with all the remaining ice cream ingredients in a blender or food processor. Process until smooth.

Pour the mixture into the baking paper-lined tray and place in the freezer for at least 4 hours to set.

Remove from the freezer, break into chunks, add to a food processor and blend until smooth.

Scoop into bowls, add your choice of toppings and serve immediately.

FUDGY COOKIE DOUGH BITES THREE WAYS

These delicious morsels taste just like traditional cookie dough without the raw egg, butter and refined white sugar. They are easy to make, filling and energy sustaining. These are my favourite three flavours but you can really play around with different ingredients. Cacao nibs give them a great crunch but you can also add crushed nuts or seeds or, if you want to get a bit fancy, you can dip the whole lot in raw melted chocky.

Makes about 12 bars
Prep time: 5 minutes (+ setting time)
Difficulty: Very easy

CHOC CHIP PEANUT BUTTER

6 medjool dates*, pitted
100 g (3½ oz/1 cup) organic rolled
   (porridge) oats*
155 g (5½ oz/1 cup) cashew nuts
1 teaspoon vanilla powder*
1 pinch salt
2 tablespoons 100% peanut butter
1 tablespoon cacao nibs*

TO SERVE
1 tablespoon cacao nibs*

CLASSIC LAMINGTON

6 medjool dates*, pitted
100 g (3½ oz/1 cup) organic rolled
   (porridge) oats*
155 g (5½ oz/1 cup) cashew nuts
1 teaspoon vanilla powder*
1 pinch salt
1 tablespoon cacao powder*
30 g (1 oz/¼ cup) dried cranberries
15 g (½ oz/¼ cup) shredded coconut

TO SERVE
2 tablespoons shredded coconut

$\rightarrow$

GINGER
& LIME

6 medjool dates*, pitted
100 g (3½ oz/1 cup) organic rolled
    (porridge) oats*
155 g (5½ oz/1 cup) cashew nuts
1 teaspoon vanilla powder*
1 pinch salt
1 tablespoon minced fresh ginger
1 lime, zested

TO SERVE
1 teaspoon lime zest

Boil 500 ml (17 fl oz/2 cups) of water and pour over the dates. Leave to soak
while you prepare the rest of the dish.

Add the oats, cashew nuts, vanilla and salt to a food processor. Pulse to
combine and blend until a flour is formed. Drain the dates and add to the food
processor with all other ingredients.

Pulse again and blend until you get a cookie-dough consistency. Mix in the
last ingredients and push evenly into a slice tin. If making the Ginger & Lime
bites, sprinkle the lime zest over the top. Place in the freezer to set for at
least 30 minutes. Slice and store in the freezer or enjoy straight away.

NUT-FREE
CHOC MOUSSE TARTS

These little bites of deliciousness are not only plant-based and free of gluten, dairy, refined sugar and egg, but they are also grain- and nut-free. And they're so easy. The mousse in these treats doesn't freeze so well and is better enjoyed fresh so here is the recipe for a small batch. Just double the recipe if you have a few more mouths to feed.

Makes about 12 small tartlets
Prep time: 20 minutes (+ setting time)
Difficulty: Easy

BASE
130 g (4½ oz/¾ cup) activated buckwheat*
45 g (1½ oz/¾ cup) shredded coconut
10 medjool dates*, pitted
1 pinch salt

FILLING
2 ripe avocados, peeled and pitted
85 ml (2¾ fl oz/⅓ cup) maple syrup*
2 tablespoons cacao powder*
½ teaspoon vanilla powder*

TO SERVE
1 tablespoon cacao nibs*
1 teaspoon dried rose petals
2 tablespoons fresh berries

In a food processor, make the bases by pulsing the buckwheat, coconut, dates and salt until a sticky texture is formed. Spoon about a tablespoon of the mixture into small silicone cupcake moulds, pressing the mixture up the sides as you go.

Place in the freezer for at least 2 hours.

Combine all the filling ingredients in a blender. Pulse to combine and blend until smooth and creamy. Remove the tart cases from the moulds and spoon the filling into each. Arrange on a platter and scatter with the cacao nibs, rose petals and berries. Enjoy!

BEETROOT, GINGER
& LIME PIE

In autumn, when beetroot (beets), lime and ginger are in season I love to make one of these pies. Beetroot has amazing cleansing properties so why not put it in a decadent dessert I say. It also gives the most amazing earthy flavour to this recipe. That, combined with the zingy freshness of the lime and ginger, is a match made in heaven.

Makes 1 large pie
Prep time: 20 minutes (+ setting time)
Difficulty: Easy

CRUST
125 g (4½ oz/1 cup) sunflower kernels

90 g (3 oz/1 cup) desiccated coconut

30 g (1 oz/¼ cup) cacao powder*

1 teaspoon vanilla powder*

10 medjool dates*, pitted

1 pinch salt

FILLING
390 g (14 oz/2½ cups) cashew nuts

105 g (3½ oz/¾ cup) beetroot (beets), grated

125 g (4½ oz/½ cup) coconut yoghurt*

185 ml (6 fl oz/¾ cup) lime juice

125 ml (4 fl oz/½ cup) maple syrup*

1 tablespoon minced fresh ginger

TO SERVE
1 teaspoon black sesame seeds

1 teaspoon white sesame seeds

Boil 750 ml (25½ fl oz/3 cups) of water and pour over the cashew nuts. Leave to soak while you prepare the crust.

Add all the crust ingredients to a food processor. Pulse to combine and process until the mixture begins to stick together.

Press into a pie case or springform cake tin.

Drain and rinse the cashew nuts. Add all the filling ingredients to a blender or food processor. Pulse to combine and blend until super smooth. Pour onto the prepared crust. Scatter with the black and white sesame seeds and place in the freezer for at least 4 hours to set.

Remove from the freezer 10–20 minutes before slicing and serving.

MINT CHOC CHIP
'ICE CREAM' SANDWICH

When we have some ripe frozen bananas in the freezer I love to make these as a treat. They are great at any time of the day. I have been known to have a few for brekkie. They are perfect on a warm summer morning and who can resist the combo of chocolate and mint?

Makes about 6 sandwiches
Prep time: 10 minutes (+ setting time)
Cook time: 15 minutes
Difficulty: Easy

COOKIE

110 g (4 oz/1 cup) chickpea flour (besan)*

1 teaspoon vanilla powder*

1 teaspoon baking powder

3 tablespoons hulled tahini*

125 ml (4 fl oz/½ cup) plant-based milk*
   (I use almond)

85 ml (2¾ fl oz/⅓ cup) maple syrup*

6 medjool dates*, pitted

2 tablespoons cacao nibs*

ICE CREAM

2 frozen bananas

2 tablespoons coconut yoghurt*

1 drop food-grade peppermint
   essential oil*

1 tablespoon cacao nibs*

Preheat the oven to 180°C (350°F) fan-forced and line a large tray with baking paper.

Add all the cookie ingredients, except the cacao nibs, to a food processor. Pulse to combine and blend until the mixture becomes a smooth dough.

Stir in the cacao nibs and roll the mixture into about 12 balls. Space evenly over the tray. Press down gently on each to make a cookie shape. Bake for 12–15 minutes or until golden brown. Allow to cool.

Meanwhile, place all the ice cream ingredients, except the cacao nibs, in a blender or food processor and blend until smooth. Add the cacao nibs and stir to combine.

Spread a generous amount of the ice cream over half of the cookies and top with the other cookies. Place in the freezer for 10 minutes to set before serving.

MUM'S APPLE, BLUEBERRY & RHUBARB CRUMBLE

As far as warming and comforting desserts go, I can't find much better than my mum's apple crumble. This recipe is adapted from hers. I have added blueberries and a bit of spice for extra warming goodness. This recipe is so full of wholefoods, flavour and sustaining energy that you could enjoy any leftovers for brekkie. It's divine to serve when it's chilly, with a big dollop of coconut yoghurt and a pinch of extra cinnamon. For a gluten-free option replace the oats with more almonds and shredded coconut. If you are planning to make this over a camp fire, pre-prepare the dry crumble mixture.

Serves 4
Prep time: 10 minutes
Cook time: 30 minutes
Difficulty: Easy

FRUIT LAYER

200 g (7 oz) apples, peeled and diced

300 g (10½ oz/2 cups) fresh or frozen blueberries

2 stalks rhubarb

2 bananas, peeled and sliced

1 tablespoon maple syrup*

juice of 1 lemon

1 teaspoon vanilla powder*

CRUMBLE LAYER

160 g (5½ oz) almonds or ground almonds

30 g (1 oz/½ cup) shredded coconut

50 g (1¾ oz/½ cup) organic rolled (porridge) oats*

2 teaspoons ground cinnamon

1 tablespoon hulled tahini*

1 tablespoon maple syrup*

TO SERVE

1 pinch of ground cinnamon

dollop of coconut yoghurt*

Preheat the oven to 200°C (400°F) fan-forced.

Heat a large saucepan on medium heat. Add all the fruit layer ingredients to the pot with 60 ml (2 fl oz/¼ cup) of water. Simmer for about 20 minutes or until the liquid begins to thicken.

Blitz the whole almonds in a food processor until a meal is formed. Combine all the dry crumble ingredients in a bowl and stir well. Add the tahini and maple syrup. Stir and crumble with your hands until evenly combined. Once the fruit is done, spread it evenly over the base of a baking dish.

Top with the crumble and place in the oven for 10-15 minutes. If you are camp-cooking, simply assemble the cooked fruit mixture and topping. Cover with foil and place close to the coals of the fire, turning carefully every now and then. Dust with the cinnamon and serve with coconut yoghurt.

TANGY PASSION, LIME &
TOASTED COCONUT 'NICE CREAM'

I have been making this super simple recipe for a few years now. The flavours are a match made in heaven. It is brimming with probiotics from the coconut yoghurt, vitamin C from the passionfruit and lime, and potassium and fibre from the bananas. It's the perfect summer brekkie, snack or after-dinner treat at the end of a long hot day.

Serves 2
Prep time: 5 minutes
Difficulty: Very easy

'NICE CREAM'
5 frozen ripe bananas, chopped
90 g (3 oz/⅓ cup) passionfruit pulp
2 tablespoons coconut yoghurt*
60 ml (2 fl oz/¼ cup) lime juice

TO SERVE
25 g (1 oz/½ cup) coconut flakes
1 tablespoon lime zest

Start by heating a non-stick frying pan over medium heat. Lightly toast the coconut flakes, keeping an eye on them to make sure they don't burn. Remove from the heat and set aside to cool.

Combine all the 'nice cream' ingredients in a food processor. Pulse to combine, then process on high speed until creamy and smooth.

Spoon into serving bowls, sprinkle with the toasted coconut flakes and lime zest and serve immediately.

PURPLE SWEET POTATO & VANILLA POPSICLES

These fuss-free pops are super creamy thanks to the sweet potato and coconut yoghurt. You can usually find purple sweet potatoes at your local grocer or farmers' market. They are white on the outside and purple on the inside, sometimes called Okinawan sweet potatoes. I love to use them not only for extra nutritional value but also to add an amazing colour to dishes, such as the Purple sweet potato smoothie bowl on page 28.

Makes about 6 popsicles
Prep time: 5 minutes (+ setting time)
Cook time: 10 minutes
Difficulty: Easy

300 g (10½ oz) purple sweet potatoes*, peeled and diced
125 g (4½ oz/½ cup) coconut yoghurt*
60 ml (2 fl oz/¼ cup) maple syrup*
1 teaspoon vanilla powder*
1 tablespoon Oaty raw-nola (see page 26)
2 teaspoons shredded coconut
edible cornflower petals (optional)

Steam the sweet potato until soft. Combine the sweet potato, coconut yoghurt, maple syrup and vanilla powder in a high-speed blender or food processor. Process until smooth.

Sprinkle a little of the oaty raw-nola, shredded coconut and, if using, cornflower petals into each popsicle mould before filling with the sweet potato mixture. Sprinkle more shredded coconut, oaty raw-nola and cornflower petals on top, add popsicle sticks and place in the freezer overnight to set.

RASPBERRY & GINGER
KOMBUCHA POPS

There is no need to feel guilty about a treat when that treat is made out of amazing ingredients, all with their own unique health benefits. These kombucha pops are super tasty and refreshing. The ginger gives them a welcome kick as well as being an amazing anti-inflammatory and digestive aid. The kombucha is full of probiotic goodness for gut health and the raspberries (which you could always swap for another variety of berry) are brimming with antioxidants.

Makes about 6 popsicles
Prep time: 10 minutes (+ freezing time)
Difficulty: Very easy

300 g (10½ oz/2 cups) frozen raspberries
250 ml (8½ fl oz/1 cup) kombucha*
1 teaspoon minced fresh ginger
zest and juice of ½ lime
1 tablespoon chia seeds*

Heat a small saucepan over very low heat. Add the frozen raspberries and gently stir until thawed and smooth. Turn the heat off. Add all the other ingredients and mix well.

When the chia starts to absorb the liquid transfer the mixture into popsicle moulds. Place popsicle sticks into each and freeze overnight.

COCONUT, BERRY &
LIME PROBIOTIC POPS

This is such a great, sneaky way to get extra probiotic goodness into your little ones. The colours are fun and the flavours are fresh. There is no waiting for layers to freeze as you can make the entire lot in one go. Most yoghurt pops or ice creams are made with loads of refined sugar, but not these. Real maple syrup, in small amounts, is a great alternative to refined white sugar as it is a minimally processed sap from the maple tree, full of vitamins and minerals. These are perfect as a cooling afternoon snack.

Makes about 8 popsicles
Prep time: 10 minutes (+ setting time)
Difficulty: Easy

RASPBERRY LAYER

110 g (4 oz/¾ cup) fresh or frozen
  raspberries
250 g (9 oz/1 cup) coconut yoghurt*
2 tablespoons maple syrup*
3 tablespoons cacao nibs*

COCONUT LAYER

125 g (4½ oz/½ cup) coconut yoghurt*

LIME LAYER

1 avocado, peeled and pitted
juice of 1 lime
2 tablespoons maple syrup*

Add all the raspberry layer ingredients to a food processor or blender. Blend until smooth. Fill about three-quarters of each popsicle mould.

Add the coconut yoghurt to create the white layer on top.

Mash the lime layer ingredients together until smooth and spoon on top of the white layer.

Place a popsicle stick into each and freeze overnight.

CHOC CHIP
CARAMEL FUDGE BROWNIES

No one will know that these are mostly made out of a root vegetable, legumes and whole grains. Did you know that black beans, one of the key ingredients in these brownies, are absolutely brimming with B6, folate, potassium and fibre? The humble black bean packs a nutrition punch and don't get me started on the old sweet potato. They are so incredibly versatile and bursting with anti-inflammatory powerhouses such as vitamins C and A. If that's not reason enough to whip up a batch of yummy brownies I don't know what is.

Makes one 13 x 23 cm (5 x 9 in) tray
Prep time: 10 minutes
Cook time: 30 minutes
Difficulty: Easy

BROWNIES

400 g (14 oz) sweet potato, peeled
   and diced
75 g (2¾ oz/¾ cup) organic rolled
   (porridge) oats*
1 teaspoon baking powder
3 tablespoons cacao powder*
¼ teaspoon salt
1 teaspoon vanilla powder*
250 g (9 oz) canned black beans, drained
   and rinsed
125 ml (4 fl oz/½ cup) maple syrup*
4 medjool dates*, pitted and diced
2 tablespoons cacao nibs*

TO SERVE

1 tablespoon freeze-dried berries
1 tablespoon dried edible flower petals

Preheat the oven to 180°C (350°F) fan-forced.

Steam the sweet potato until soft.

Process the oats in a food processor until a flour is formed. Add the baking powder, cacao powder, salt and vanilla. Lightly pulse to combine. Add the sweet potato, black beans and maple syrup and blend until smooth.

Stir in the chopped dates and half the cacao nibs. Pour into a baking paper-lined tray, spreading the mixture all the way to the edges.

Sprinkle with the remaining cacao nibs and bake for 30 minutes.

Remove from the oven and allow to cool for 20–30 minutes before slicing and sprinkling with the freeze-dried berries and flower petals. Nuts also work a treat as a garnish for this one.

GINGER
BERRY KISSES

Chewy, spicy and delicious, these cookies are so moreish. The main ingredient is chickpea flour, or besan, which is basically dried chickpeas, ground into a flour. Who knew it would make such perfect ginger cookies? It is just a bonus that they are so simple to make. You can top them with any frozen berries you like. Blueberries and strawberries both work well but I just can't go past raspberries. I think these kisses are best enjoyed straight out of the oven with a glass of ice-cold almond milk.

Makes about 8 cookies
Prep time: 5 minutes
Cook time: 15 minutes
Difficulty: Easy

110 g (4 oz/1 cup) chickpea flour (besan)*

1 teaspoon vanilla powder*

1 teaspoon ground cinnamon

½ teaspoon baking powder

1 pinch salt

1 tablespoon hulled tahini*

1 tablespoon minced fresh ginger

8 medjool dates*, pitted

35 g (1¼ oz/¼ cup) frozen berries

Preheat the oven to 180°C (350°F) fan-forced.

Line a baking tray with baking paper.

Combine all the dry ingredients in a food processor and pulse to combine. Add the tahini, ginger and dates and blend until a dough is formed.

Press a few frozen berries into each cookie. Place in the oven to bake for 10 minutes. Allow to cool, then serve.

SALTED CARAMEL
ESPRESSO SWIRL 'CHEESECAKE'

It doesn't get much better than coffee in cake form. This cake tastes as good as it looks, if not better. The filling is creamy, the base is sweet and crunchy and the caramel swirl is smooth with just the slightest hint of saltiness. Talk about balance. It's all in the quality of the ingredients, as usual. Organic is best. I like to take a ceramic mug down to our local cafe to grab a few shots of espresso from them for the cake. It always results in the best flavour.

Serves about 12
Prep time: 30 minutes (+ setting time)
Difficulty: Medium

BASE
155 g (5½ oz/1 cup) raw almonds
8 medjool dates*, pitted

CARAMEL ESPRESSO SWIRL
10 medjool dates*, pitted
60 ml (2 fl oz/¼ cup) espresso
1 tablespoon hulled tahini*
¼ teaspoon salt
¼ teaspoon vanilla powder*

FILLING
460 g (1 lb/3 cups) cashew nuts
125 ml (4 fl oz/½ cup) maple syrup*
60 ml (2 fl oz/¼ cup) plant-based milk*
60 ml (2 fl oz/¼ cup) espresso
1 teaspoon vanilla powder*
1 pinch salt

Pour near-boiling water over the dates for the swirl and leave to soak.

Cover the cashew nuts in near-boiling water also and leave to soak while you prepare the base.

Combine the base ingredients in a food processor and pulse until you get a sticky consistency.

Press the mixture into a cake or slice tin lined with baking paper.

To make the filling, drain and rinse the cashew nuts. Blend all the filling ingredients on high speed in a blender or food processor until smooth and creamy. Pour over the base.

Drain the dates. Add all the remaining caramel espresso swirl ingredients to a blender or food processor, pulse to combine and blend until smooth.

Pour evenly into the tin in a swirl pattern and, using a chopstick, gently stir the mixture in, making small figure eight motions.

Place in the freezer for a minimum of 4 hours to set. Remove 10-15 minutes before slicing and serving.

DRINKS

NOURISHING BROTH

You can use this light and nourishing broth as a base for your soups and stir-fries or as a warm, comforting drink all on its own. Wakame is an edible seaweed and you can usually find it at Asian grocers or your local wholefood or health food store. Wakame is a good source of calcium, magnesium, iron and iodine. The miso provides another amazing element to this broth.

Makes 2 litres (68 fl oz)
Prep time: 10 minutes
Cook time: 1 hour
Difficulty: Easy

BROTH

10 g (¼ oz) dried wakame*

1 large leek, white part only, finely shredded

4 garlic cloves, minced

1 tablespoon minced fresh ginger

2 teaspoons fresh turmeric

4 stalks celery, thinly sliced

1 litre (34 fl oz/4 cups) vegetable stock

1 litre (34 fl oz/4 cups) filtered water

3 tablespoons coconut aminos*

1 large beetroot (beet), peeled and thinly sliced

60 g (2 oz/2 cups) flat-leaf (Italian) parsley, chopped

45 g (1½ oz/1 cup) kale or English spinach, chopped

2 tablespoons miso*

Start by placing the dried wakame in a bowl of water to reconstitute it while you prepare the rest of the dish.

In a saucepan, sauté the leek, garlic, ginger, turmeric and celery in a little vegetable stock until soft. Drain the water from the wakame, and add the wakame to the sautéed vegetables along with the rest of the vegetable stock, the filtered water, coconut aminos and beetroot.

Bring to the boil, then reduce to a simmer and cook for 45 minutes. Add the parsley, kale and miso, stirring well. Continue to simmer for a further 5 minutes.

Strain to separate the broth or serve as a light soup with the veggies.

Alternatively, if you have a slow cooker you can combine all the ingredients and cook for 12 hours or more, adding the greens and miso at the very end.

KOMBUCHA
MOCKTAILS THREE WAYS

When I was in my early teens, Mum had this odd stuff bubbling away in batches on the kitchen bench. She would ask us all to have a small amount each day and, to begin with, I have to admit it was quite a rude shock. This was well before kombucha became as popular as it is today and we had not heard of mixing it with other tasty fruits and spices to create a refreshing drink. I still don't love the stuff straight up, but I enjoy it naturally flavoured in a super tasty way. These fresh and yummy kombucha mocktails are no exception to that rule. I hope you love them too.

Serves 2
Prep time: 5 minutes
Difficulty: Very easy

BLUEBERRY, GINGER & THYME

1 teaspoon juiced fresh ginger
juice of ½ lime
2 tablespoons fresh blueberries
150 g (5½ oz/1 cup) crushed ice
375 ml (12½ fl oz/1½ cups) hibiscus kombucha*

TO SERVE
2 thyme sprigs

RASPBERRY MOJITO

35 g (1¼ oz/¼ cup) raspberries, mashed
1 tablespoon finely chopped mint
juice of ½ lime
1 lime slice
150 g (5½ oz/1 cup) crushed ice
375 ml (12½ fl oz/1½ cups) kombucha*

TO SERVE
2 rosemary sprigs

CUCUMBER &
GREEN APPLE

½ cucumber, juiced
1 green apple, juiced
juice of ½ lemon
150 g (5½ oz/1 cup) crushed ice
250 ml (8½ fl oz/1 cup) kombucha*

TO SERVE
2 slices cucumber

Combine all the ingredients, except for the ice and kombucha, in the bottom of a tall glass.

Stir well. Add the crushed ice and pour over the kombucha. Serve with a slice of cucumber.

TURMERIC & GINGER
SPARKLING PREBIOTIC

Apple-cider vinegar is the prebiotic in this sweet and slightly sour drink. Prebiotics are important as they feed probiotics, the good microflora in your digestive system. I like to use a little maple syrup as the sweetener to balance out the vinegar, but you can omit this if you like. The turmeric and ginger are both anti-inflammatory, so this makes for a pretty special sparkling drink. Serve with ice, passionfruit, berries or any other trimmings.

Serves 2
Prep time: 2 minutes
Difficulty: Very easy

¼ teaspoon ground turmeric

¼ teaspoon ground ginger

1 tablespoon apple-cider vinegar*

½ teaspoon maple syrup*

500 ml (17 fl oz/2 cups) sparkling water, chilled

Combine the turmeric, ginger, apple-cider vinegar and maple syrup in a tall glass.

Whisk together with a fork. Add the ice and slowly fill with sparking water.

BREKKIE
THICKIES FOUR WAYS

These babies will keep you going for ages. The sustaining oats, chia, and fats in the coconut yoghurt make a hearty base. Any plant-based milk will work well. I use either almond or coconut milk as I think they provide the best creamy flavour and texture. These make such a perfect brekkie on the go and are full of colour and nourishing wholefoods.

Serves 1
Prep time: 2 minutes
Difficulty: Very easy

CHOC
COCONUT

2 frozen bananas

25 g (1 oz/¼ cup) organic rolled (porridge) oats*

1 teaspoon chia seeds*

2 teaspoons cacao powder*

½ teaspoon vanilla powder*

2 teaspoons cacao nibs*

2 tablespoons coconut yoghurt*

60 ml (2 fl oz/¼ cup) plant-based milk*

TO SERVE

2 tablespoons coconut yoghurt*

1 teaspoon cacao nibs*

BERRY
DELICIOUS

75 g (2¾ oz/½ cup) frozen mango chunks

75 g (2¾ oz/½ cup) frozen berries

25 g (1 oz/¼ cup) organic rolled (porridge) oats*

1 teaspoon chia seeds*

juice of 1 lime

2 tablespoons coconut yoghurt*

60 ml (2 fl oz/¼ cup) plant-based milk*

TO SERVE

1 teaspoon lime zest

PASSIONFRUIT & TURMERIC

1 passionfruit
2 frozen bananas
25 g (1 oz/¼ cup) organic rolled
   (porridge) oats*
1 teaspoon chia seeds*
juice of 1 lemon
½ teaspoon ground turmeric
2 tablespoons coconut yoghurt*
125 ml (4 fl oz/½ cup) plant-based milk*

TO SERVE
1 passionfruit
½ teaspoon desiccated coconut*

SUPER GREENIE

100 g (3½ oz/¾ cup) frozen mango chunks
45 g (1½ oz/1 cup) English spinach
25 g (1 oz/¼ cup) organic rolled (porridge)
   oats*
1 teaspoon chia seeds*
juice of 1 lime
2 tablespoons coconut yoghurt*
60 ml (2 fl oz/¼ cup) plant-based milk*

TO SERVE
2 mint sprigs

Place all the ingredients in a high-speed blender. Pulse to combine and blend until super smooth and creamy.

Sprinkle with your choice of toppings. Alternatively, you could layer the coconut yoghurt in with the Choc coconut smoothie, or the passionfruit in with the Passionfruit & turmeric smoothie.

SPICED CHAI,
TURMERIC & GINGER ELIXIR

This anti-inflammatory delight is warm and comforting on a brisk winter's day, or yummy served over ice on a warm summer's day. I like to use an organic, caffeine-free chai that I pick up from my local health food store, but regular chai will also do the trick. Every sip feels like it is doing you the world of good. To make the iced version simply fill a tall glass with ice and 125 ml (4 fl oz/½ cup) of almond or coconut milk. Pour the simmered spices over the milk and ice and serve immediately.

Serves 1
Prep time: 2 minutes
Cook time: 10 minutes
Difficulty: Easy

1 teaspoon finely grated fresh turmeric

½ teaspoon ground cinnamon

2 teaspoons minced fresh ginger

2 teaspoons loose leaf caffeine-free chai tea

375 ml (12½ fl oz/1½ cups) plant-based milk*

1 teaspoon maple syrup*

Bring 125 ml (4 fl oz/½ cup) of water to the boil and reduce to a simmer. Add the turmeric, cinnamon, ginger and chai. Simmer for 5 minutes. Add your plant-based milk of choice. Simmer for a further 5 minutes. Strain into a mug and stir in a little maple syrup. If you have a milk frother you can use this to create a frothy latte.

BASICS

OATY
SEED LOAF

No 'airy fairy' bread here. This loaf of hearty, tasty, seeded goodness is yummy and so easy to make. No waiting for dough to rise, no yeast, refined flours or oil. You can also make it into rolls by baking individual buns. I like to slice mine and store them in the freezer so that I always have some on hand. A little goes a long way with this hearty loaf. It is super satisfying toasted and served with soup, used as a roll for a veggie burger or topped with tasty toast toppings. For a nourishing fruit loaf, add dried fruit and spices. There are so many options.

Makes 1 large loaf
Prep time: 5 minutes
Cook time: 1 hour
Difficulty: Easy

300 g (10½ oz/3 cups) organic rolled (porridge) oats*
60 g (2 oz/½ cup) chia seeds*
40 g (1½ oz/½ cup) psyllium husks
70 g (2½ oz/½ cup) pepitas (pumpkin seeds)
60 g (2 oz/½ cup) sunflower kernels
80 g (2¾ oz/½ cup) sesame seeds
1 tablespoon linseeds (flax seeds)
1 teaspoon salt
1 teaspoon baking powder
1 tablespoon maple syrup*
500 ml (17 fl oz/2 cups) warm water

Preheat the oven to 180°C (350°F) fan-forced.

Combine all the dry ingredients in a bowl and mix well.

Stir the maple syrup and warm water together and add to the dry ingredients. Mix well. Let stand for a few minutes.

Line a loaf tin with baking paper and transfer the mixture to the tin. Spread evenly with a spatula.

Place in the oven to bake for 30 minutes.

Remove from the tin, flip upside down and bake for a further 30–40 minutes.

Leave to cool before cutting.

Store in the fridge for up to 1 week.

NUT-FREE
CHOCKY SPREAD

You will not believe how easy this chocky spread is to make. You will want to eat it by the spoon but I think the best way to enjoy it is on the Oaty seed loaf from page 254, toasted over an open fire. It is a great recipe to take camping and is also really yummy on pancakes.

Makes 1 cup
Prep time: 2 minutes
Difficulty: Very easy

200 g (7 oz/¾ cup) hulled tahini*
60 ml (2 fl oz/¼ cup) maple syrup*
2 tablespoons cacao powder*
1 teaspoon vanilla powder*

Whisk the tahini and maple syrup together in a bowl. Add the dry ingredients and mix well. You can also do this in a food processor.

Pour into a sterilised glass jar and store in the fridge for up to 2 weeks.

SWEET
CHILLI AÏOLI

There may be a little soaking to do for this recipe, but let's face it, that involves putting something in water, walking away and forgetting about it. And it is so worth it. The result is the most creamy, tangy, sweet and spicy aïoli. You can make a batch on a weeknight to last the whole week. It can be used in so many ways: on wraps, in toasted sandwiches, on salads and as a dip. Very worth soaking a few cashew nuts.

Makes 1½ cups
Prep time: 5 minutes (+ soaking time)
Difficulty: Very easy

155 g (5½ oz/1 cup) cashew nuts, soaked
    in water for 8 hours
zest and juice of ½ lemon
2 teaspoons apple-cider vinegar*
2 teaspoons garlic powder
½ teaspoon salt
85 ml (2¾ fl oz/⅓ cup) water
1 teaspoon maple syrup*
1 large red chilli, sliced

Drain and rinse the cashew nuts well. Add to a blender or food processor with all the other ingredients. Pulse to combine and blend until super smooth.

Serve with wedges, or as a tasty, spicy salad dressing.

Store in the fridge for up to 1 week.

CASHEW 'NOTZZARELLA'

This plant-based version of traditional mozzarella cheese has revolutionised pizza night at our house. Not only that, dollops of this creamy, easy-to-make cheese can be added to many dishes. It spreads well on toast, or on savoury crackers and is perfect in wraps. I like to freeze any leftovers when I make a batch. You do have to wait for it to thaw again but that can sometimes be easier than making a fresh batch. Another way we love to enjoy this cheese is in a simple Insalata caprese with olives (see page 102). So good.

Makes 1 cup
Prep time: 10 minutes
Cook time: 10 minutes
Difficulty: Easy

155 g (5½ oz/1 cup) cashew nuts
50 g (1¾ oz/⅓ cup) tapioca flour
20 g (¾ oz/⅓ cup) nutritional yeast*
½ teaspoon salt
juice of 1 lemon

Pour boiling water over the cashew nuts and leave to soak for 10 minutes.

Place an empty shallow bowl in the freezer to chill.

Drain and rinse the soaked cashew nuts.

Combine all the ingredients in a blender or food processor. Add 375 ml (12½ fl oz/ 1½ cups) of water and blend until smooth. Transfer to a saucepan over medium heat. Gently simmer and stir until the mixture thickens. Continue to stir until the mixture is thick and pliable. Set aside to cool for 10 minutes.

Remove the bowl from the freezer and spread the mixture over the base. Place the bowl of mixture in the freezer for 10 minutes.

Pull the 'notzzarella' apart to add to pizzas, salads or allow to come to room temperature before using it as a spread.

Store in an airtight container in the fridge for up to 1 week or freeze for longer periods.

WHITE BEAN PESTO

This pesto is super quick and easy to make. It is tasty, light and filling all at once. I like to enjoy it spread thickly on toast, in a wrap with some roast veg or just as a scrumptious, simple dip. It's thick so it makes a good option to take on the go in your lunchbox and add to your salads. It's also yummy on baked spuds with some Cashew 'parmesan' (see page 272) and greens, or added to any nourish bowl (see the Bowls chapter).

Makes 2 cups
Prep time: 5 minutes
Difficulty: Very easy

PESTO

500 g (1 lb 2 oz) canned cannellini (lima)
   beans, drained and rinsed
juice of 1 lemon
120 g (4 oz/2 cups) parsley, chopped
20 g (¾ oz/⅓ cup) nutritional yeast*
2 teaspoons garlic powder
2 tablepoons coconut aminos*
½ teaspoon salt

TO SERVE

Corn tortilla chips (see page 172) or pita
parsley
1 tablespoon pine nuts, toasted

Add all the pesto ingredients to a blender. Pulse to combine and blend until smooth.

Serve with the tortilla chips or pita and top with the parsley and pine nuts.

Store in an airtight container in the fridge.

QUICK
PICKLED ONION

I originally made this pickled onion to use up some red onion I had on hand and it was so good I have made it many times since. It is a great way to add that tangy vinegar flavour (as well as some vibrant colour) to salads, burgers and wraps.

Makes 1 cup
Prep time: 2 minutes (+ pickling time)
Difficulty: Very easy

1 red onion
185 ml (6 fl oz/¾ cup) red-wine vinegar
¼ teaspoon salt

Very thinly slice the onion using a mandoline, sharp knife or spiraliser. Gently squeeze the onion until softened.

Place the onion, vinegar and salt in a bowl, ensuring the onion is covered. Set aside to pickle for about 30 minutes. To serve, drain the liquid or use a fork to remove the onion. Keep the liquid to store any leftover onion in an airtight container in the fridge for up to 1 week.

MISO
HUMMUS

I cannot imagine a world without hummus. It is so versatile and always satisfying. You may already have most of the ingredients on hand. I like to add it to salads, wraps and enjoy it as a yummy dip. The miso in this version provides the salty flavour with extra probiotics. I try to buy fresh organic miso from the fridge section of my local health food store.

Makes about 2 cups
Prep time: 10 minutes
Difficulty: Very easy

HUMMUS

3 garlic cloves, minced

zest and juice of 2 lemons

500 g (1 lb 2 oz) canned chickpeas,
    drained and rinsed

4 tablespoons hulled tahini*

2 tablespoons miso*

½ teaspoon chilli powder

125 ml (4 fl oz/½ cup) water

TO SERVE

1 pinch smoked paprika*

1 teaspoon sesame seeds

1 parsley sprig

Place the minced garlic in a small bowl and cover with lemon juice while you prepare the rest of the dish.

Combine the remaining hummus ingredients in a high-speed blender. Pulse to combine and blend until super smooth and creamy, adding more water if needed. Serve with the smoked paprika, sesame seeds and parsley or store in an airtight container in the fridge for up to 1 week.

FRESH
SALSA

Nothing beats the flavour of good-quality, in-season fresh fruits and veggies, especially of the home-grown variety. Tomatoes are no exception and the quality of the tomatoes you use for this salsa will make all the difference. Choose organic where possible. The richness in colour and flavour will lift the whole meal or platter. I love adding this fresh, yummy salsa to any Mexican-style dish I make.

Makes 1½ cups
Prep time: 5 minutes
Difficulty: Very easy

225 g (8 oz) cherry tomatoes

1 red capsicum (bell pepper)

⅓ red onion

1 tablespoon coriander (cilantro) leaves

1 tablespoon coconut aminos*

juice of 1 small lime

Finely dice the cherry tomatoes, capsicum, and onion. Chop the coriander. Combine all the ingredients in a bowl and stir well. Serve immediately or store in an airtight container in the fridge.

SPICED
CHICKPEAS

These are a favourite staple of mine. I add them to salads for extra flavour and texture. Combine them in nourish bowls (see the Bowls chapter). Top soups with them or enjoy as a tasty addition to a plant-based platter.

Makes 1½ cups
Prep time: 2 minutes
Cook time: 15 minutes
Difficulty: Very easy

250 g (9 oz) canned chickpeas, drained and rinsed
1½ tablespoons coconut aminos*
2 teaspoons smoked paprika*
1 teaspoon garlic powder
½ teaspoon ground ginger
½ teaspoon ground cumin
½ teaspoon chilli powder
½ teaspoon salt

Preheat the oven to 180°C (350°F) fan-forced.

Line a large baking tray with baking paper.

Combine all the ingredients in a bowl and stir until evenly combined.

Spread out on the oven tray and place in the oven to bake for 10 minutes.

Remove from the oven and stir well before baking for a further 5 minutes.

Can be stored in an airtight container in the fridge.

CASHEW 'PARMESAN'

I have not missed the traditional version since discovering this scrumptious plant-based version of parmesan. It takes next to no time to whip up and is so yummy on pizza, pasta, salads and in wraps. I like to store mine in a glass jar in the fridge to keep it fresh and ready to add to my meals. It keeps in the fridge for up to two weeks. Freeze to store for longer periods.

Makes 1 cup
Prep time: 2 minutes
Difficulty: Very easy

155 g (5½ oz/1 cup) raw cashew nuts
20 g (¾ oz/⅓ cup) nutritional yeast*
1 teaspoon garlic powder
1 teaspoon salt

Add all the ingredients to a food processor. Pulse until you get a texture like ground almonds.

Store in an airtight container in the fridge for up to 2 weeks or freeze for longer periods.

'CHEESY'
TAHINI SAUCE

Despite its simplicity, this sauce took a while to perfect. It's all in the balance of the basic ingredients that give it that delicious rich flavour without being too heavy. You can store any leftovers in the fridge for a couple of days but I doubt there will be any left!

Makes about 1 cup
Prep time: 2 minutes
Difficulty: Very easy

125 ml (4 fl oz/½ cup) plant-based milk*
   (I use almond milk)
30 g (1 oz/½ cup) nutritional yeast*
2 tablespoons hulled tahini*
1 teaspoon garlic powder
½ teaspoon salt

Add all the ingredients to a food processor. Pulse to combine and blend until smooth and creamy.

Store in an airtight container in the fridge.

TANGY
MISO SAUCE

Umami, the beautiful Japanese word for savoury taste, is balanced perfectly in this sauce with sweetness, sourness, bitterness and saltiness. The sauce can be added to salads and nourish bowls (see the Bowls chapter), used as a dipping sauce or stirred through noodles and veggies to make a scrumptious Tangy Thai kelp noodle salad (see page 88). I highly recommend sourcing a good-quality brand of authentic miso from the fridge section of your health food store. It will make all the difference to the flavour of this sauce.

Makes 1 cup
Prep time: 10 minutes
Difficulty: Very easy

juice of 1 lemon

1 teaspoon garlic powder

2 tablespoons miso*

2 tablespoons hulled tahini*

2 tablespoons coconut aminos*

coriander (cilantro) leaves, to serve

Add all the ingredients to a blender. Pulse to combine and blend until smooth. Store in a glass jar in the fridge for up to 1 week. Serve garnished with coriander leaves.

Store in an airtight container in the fridge for up to 1 week.

SMOKY
COCONUT 'BACON'

This tasty 'bacon' substitute is ready in only ten minutes and adds extra flavour and texture to just about any dish. It's made of only three ingredients. I recommend making a big enough batch for snacking as well as adding to your meals. Trust me, it's so moreish you will need to. Use in place of bacon in any dish. Store in an airtight container in the freezer. No need to thaw.

Makes 1½ cups
Prep time: 2 minutes
Cook time: 10 minutes
Difficulty: Very easy

75 g (2¾ oz/1½ cups) coconut flakes
2 tablespoons coconut aminos*
1 tablespoon smoked paprika*

Preheat the oven to 180°C (350°F) fan-forced.

Combine the coconut flakes and coconut aminos in a bowl and fold gently until the coconut is evenly coated. Add the smoked paprika and toss to combine.

Line a large baking tray with baking paper and evenly spread the mixture over the tray.

Bake in the oven for 10 minutes. Remove from the oven and gently stir on the tray. The coconut should turn a dark caramel colour. Set aside to cool and crisp before enjoying.

Store in an airtight container in the fridge for up to 1 week.

PLANT-BASED PANTRY

These are some of the items I find very useful in plant-based cooking.
They are marked with * in the ingredients lists.

Activated buckwheat

The seeds from the buckwheat plant. The activating process involves soaking, washing and dehydrating, which removes the phytic acid and unlocks the seeds' nutrients. You can activate buckwheat yourself, but nowadays there is pre-activated buckwheat readily available from many health food stores, supermarkets, specialist grocers and online.

Apple-cider vinegar

A prebiotic vinegar, made from fermenting crushed apples until no sugars remain. It is widely used in tonics and recipes. Look for apple-cider vinegar that is raw or contains 'the mother'. Available from many wholefood stores, grocers and supermarkets.

Black bean spaghetti

A great alternative to regular wheat pasta. It is gluten-free and made from minimal ingredients, tender and brimming with protein. There are a few brands of organic black bean spaghetti available. You will find most of them at health food or wholefood stores and online.

Cacao nibs

Dried seeds of the cacao bean. Brimming with antioxidants and magnesium. I like to use them as a wholefood alternative to chocolate chips as they add a great crunch. You can now find ethically sourced product at wholefood and health food stores as well as some grocers and online.

Cacao powder

The raw form of cocoa powder, giving it a much higher antioxidant content. Delicious added to desserts, sauces and smoothies for a rich chocolate flavour. Many stores now stock ethically sourced cacao, including health food stores, wholefood stores and online.

Chia seeds

An ancient seed native to southern Mexico and Guatemala. High in omega-3 fatty acids. Used in plant-based cooking as a substitute for egg. Chia is grown in abundance here in Australia and widely available at supermarkets, health food stores, wholefood stores, at grocers and online.

Chickpea flour

Also known as besan. Made from whole ground chickpeas. A versatile ingredient that can be used to make anything from pizza bases or cookies to cakes and slices. Naturally loaded with fibre, protein, B vitamins and potassium. You can find it in most wholefood and health food stores as well as online and in a few supermarkets.

Coconut aminos

The fermented liquid made from the aged sap of the coconut blossom, with a sweet, salty, tangy flavour. Often used as a lower-sodium substitute for soy sauce or tamari. I also like to use it to replace oil and vinegar and add flavour to many of the recipes in this book. Find it at most health food and wholefood stores as well as specialist grocers.

Coconut yoghurt

Made from cultured coconut milk and containing loads of good bacteria, this is a creamy plant-based replacement for dairy yoghurt and cream. I have a simple recipe on the Natural Harry blog. Making it yourself is a great way to save a few dollars and also plastic. Find organic brands at health food stores, wholefood stores and some grocers.

Food-grade essential oil

A pure and very potent oil. Only a few varieties and brands are certified organic and suitable for dietary use. The flavours I use most often are orange and peppermint. A little goes a very long way, so you only need the tiniest amount. You can find food-grade essential oils online and in some health food stores.

Kelp noodles

Made from sea kelp, sodium and water, these are naturally gluten- and grain-free. They are rich in nutrients and can be eaten raw or soaked in water to soften. You can find them at most health food and wholefood stores as well as some specialist grocers and online.

Kimchi

Traditionally a staple condiment of Korean cuisine. Made by fermenting Napa cabbages, radishes, chilli, ginger, garlic, onion and salt. The result is absolutely bursting with flavour. Kimchi contains beneficial bacteria to support a healthy gut. I look for brands that don't contain anchovies. You can find it at many health food and wholefood stores as well as some specialist grocers. Or make a big batch yourself.

Kombucha

A lightly effervescent tea due to its fermentation process involving tea, sugar and a symbiotic colony of bacteria and yeast, which digests the sugar in the tea so trace amounts remain. The result is a slightly sour, slightly sweet, lightly fizzy tea that is most commonly enjoyed chilled. It is an ancient drink that has become increasingly popular in recent years, and is now widely available. Make it at home or find it at health food and wholefood stores.

Maple syrup

Real, pure maple syrup is made from the sap of Canadian maple trees. Unlike refined white sugar, maple syrup retains all of its vitamins and minerals after its minimal processing, which involves evaporation, making it a great natural sweetener. You can find real maple syrup at wholefood stores, health food stores, organic grocers and most supermarkets.

Medjool dates

They are super sweet and packed with fibre, and contain magnesium, copper, potassium and manganese. Medjool dates make a fantastic wholefood alternative to sugar and work really well in desserts to bind ingredients together. Medjool dates are readily available in supermarkets, and organic varieties are available at most health food stores, wholefood stores and specialty grocers.

Miso

A traditional Japanese seasoning made by fermenting rice, soy beans, salt and koji starter. Naturally high in protein, probiotics, vitamins and minerals. A traditional, non-pasteurised miso has quite a sweet and salty flavour. Luckily there are now a few good-quality Australian brands available that are made from fresh organic ingredients maintaining the probiotics. These are available from some organic grocers, health food and wholefood stores.

Mung bean fettuccine

A hearty gluten-free, wholefood pasta made from edamame and mung beans. High in potassium, manganese, folate, magnesium, zinc and B vitamins. It is also high in fibre and protein and holds its shape really well, making it a great option to add to salads. You can find it at some health food stores, wholefood stores and online.

Nori

An edible seaweed that is rack-dried in sheets. Most commonly used as a wrapping for sushi. Nori is high in vitamins and minerals, including iodine, and is best sourced organically. You can find organic toasted nori sheets at many health food and wholefood stores as well as organic grocers.

Nutritional yeast

Sometimes called savoury yeast. It is an inactive yeast grown on molasses. It is then washed and dried with heat to make sure it is inactive. Nutritional yeast is what I use to give recipes that savoury, 'cheesy' flavour. It is also a source of vitamin B12, folic acid, selenium, zinc and protein. Nutritional yeast is becoming more widely available all the time. Currently you can find it in most health food and wholefood stores as well as organic grocers and online.

Organic rolled (porridge) oats

Although oats are not a very exotic grain and are very common here in Australia, they are actually a very healthy choice. They are rich in a certain type of dietary fibre called beta-glucan as well as protein, good carbohydrates, magnesium and zinc. You can find organic rolled oats at most supermarkets, health food and wholefood stores.

Plant-based milk

You can derive milk from some nuts, seeds and grains, such as coconut, almonds, cashew nuts, rice and oats. They are relatively simple to make yourself at home, but so many are now easy to find at your local health food or wholefood store as well as most major supermarkets.

Purple sweet potato

Also known as Okinawan sweet potato, as it is popular and widely used on the Japanese island of Okinawa, these have white skin and purple flesh. They are super high in many nutrients including the obvious - fibre - and a great way to add a bit of extra colour to your meal. You can find them in some specialty grocers, farmers' markets and some wholefood stores.

Sauerkraut

A traditional German condiment made by fermenting cabbage and salt. The tangy, salty preserve is naturally probiotic. I have two basic recipes on the Natural Harry blog and they are very easy to make. These days it is readily available at many health food stores, wholefood stores and organic grocers.

Smoked paprika

A spice made from pimiento peppers that have been dried, smoked over an oak fire and ground into a fine powder. Adding this spice to recipes gives them a yummy smoky quality. You can find great-quality versions at specialty grocers, health food and wholefood stores.

Tahini

The paste produced from ground sesame seeds. Hulled tahini has a smooth and creamy texture with a very distinct nutty flavour. I have used hulled tahini in these recipes for a milder flavour. You can find hulled, unhulled and black tahini in most major supermarkets, health food stores and wholefood stores.

Tamari

A naturally gluten-free by-product of fermented soy beans. Traditionally made as a by-product of miso. It is very high in sodium and only a little is needed for a lot of flavour. Be sure to look for a brand that has no additives. You can find authentic tamari at many health food and wholefood stores as well as specialist grocers.

Tempeh

A naturally cultured soy product. The controlled fermentation process binds the soy beans together. Tempeh is a great source of protein, and is delicious grilled, in sandwiches, salads, wraps, curry and stir-fries. As with all soy products it is best to source high-quality organic brands. You can find these at many organic grocers, wholefood and health food stores.

Tofu

Also known as bean curd, tofu is available in a few forms: silken, firm, extra firm and smoked. Tofu, in its organic, non-GMO form is a great source of amino acids, iron and calcium. You can usually find a good-quality organic tofu at health food stores, wholefood stores and some specialist grocers.

Vanilla powder

Made by grinding dehydrated whole vanilla bean pods. Be sure to look at the ingredients though. Some of the brands have added sugar for baking. Vanilla bean should be the only ingredient. You can find organic vanilla powder in most wholefood and health food stores as well as online.

Wakame

An edible sea vegetable. I like to use it in soups and salads. As with many other edible sea vegetables, wakame is super high in many nutrients and a great source of iodine. You can find organic dehydrated wakame at many health food stores and wholefood stores as well as online.

INDEX

THANK YOU

First, the biggest, warmest heartfelt thank you to Nikole Ramsay, who has magically captured every image in this beautiful book. I first met Nikole when I provided a plant-based wedding cake for an editorial that Nikole was photographing. Watching Nikole work that day I witnessed so much professionalism and watched her produce the most beautiful photos I had ever seen. So, when I began my first recipe book and needed a photographer that really understood Natural Harry, I didn't need to look any further. Nikole, a Barwon Heads local, was such a major part of the last book it was natural that she became an even bigger part of this book. Nik has worked with me on many aspects of this book, including absorbing herself in recipe testing. Nik, your bright, sunny and perfectly balanced photographs match your personality and it is always such a privilege to collaborate with you!

To Frase, my better half as they say. One incredibly grounded, clever, kind, hard-working, innovative, fun and creative human. Thank you for the adventures we have had so far, and for inspiring so much of this book. Thank you for dreaming up crazy ideas with me and always being open to all the possibilities. Thank you for being my resident recipe tester, always. You are the biggest legend I know.

It would be remiss of me to not thank my treasured family and extended family, my friends. A list of names of people that mean the world to me could fill another book. I feel like the luckiest girl in the world when I think of each and every one of you and though you may not know it, all of you have contributed to or inspired this book in some way through adventures together, chats enjoyed over food, messages and phone calls.

Thank you to Amanda for being the world's best recipe tester. You are one of a kind and a true bright spark. Jessie, thank you for your hours of listening and for your help untangling my somewhat jumbled words. Your patience and calm presence was exactly the energy I needed at the eleventh hour. To Jessie, Clarey, Soph and Sammy, my lady surfing buddies. Thank you for all the fun paddles and expert second opinions on these recipes.

One very important person I now owe the world to is Caroline Adams, whose years of experience and generous spirit have kept my written ramblings at bay in not only these pages but those of the last book too. A big thank you to Penny Cordner and Tim Dowling also for all your help!

To those who I call the 'photo shoot legends' for giving their valuable time, and bringing the laughter to the crazy photo shoot days. To Alice my amazing 'floralising' friend and her cute little sidekick, Peggy, for being the best prop managers and keeping me grounded when I felt like I needed another eight arms to get it all done! Jade, for keeping everyone in check, on time and for your amazing videography skills. Katie, the gorgeous blondie in some of these pages who began as one of the smoothie crew in the caravan and has since become a treasured friend! Jarryd, for your picnic-eating and hanging-out skills and for being so agreeable and such a legend! To Abbey, it has been such a pleasure to get to know you. I feel like we speak the same language and I cannot wait to create some amazing things together in the future.

Thank you to the extended Natural Harry family. To every single social media and email subscriber, stockist and business that I have had the pleasure to know. Thank you for your continued support, well wishes, comments and correspondence. It is crazy the amount of wonderful human beings I have met through the experience of Natural Harry. We all crave connection and community in our lives and I am truly grateful for this one, so thank you.

Lastly, I would like to extend an enormous amount of gratitude your way. Producing a second recipe book was a dream of mine and Nikole's but it was also a massive leap of faith yet again so thank you. Thank you for buying a copy, gifting it to someone special and spreading the word!

X Harry

Oven temperatures are for fan-forced ovens; if you have a conventional oven, increase the temperature by 20°C (35°F).

This book uses 20 ml (¾ fl oz) tablespoons; cooks using 15 ml (½ fl oz) tablespoons should be generous with their tablespoon measurements. Metric cup measurements are used, i.e. 250 ml (8½ fl oz) for 1 cup; in the US a cup is 237 ml (8 fl oz), so American cooks should be generous with their cup measurements; in the UK, a cup is 284 ml (9½ fl oz), so British cooks should be scant with their cup measurements.

This edition published in 2018 by Hardie Grant Books,
an imprint of Hardie Grant Publishing
First published in 2017 by Harriet Birrell

Hardie Grant Books (Melbourne)
Building 1, 658 Church Street
Richmond, Victoria 3121

Hardie Grant Books (London)
5th & 6th Floors
52-54 Southwark Street
London SE1 1UN

hardiegrantbooks.com

 A catalogue record for this book is available from the National Library of Australia

NATIONAL LIBRARY OF AUSTRALIA

Whole
ISBN 978 1 74379 516 3

10 9 8 7 6 5 4 3 2

Publishing Director: Jane Willson
Project Editor: Loran McDougall
Editor & Designer: Harriet Birrell
Photographer: Nikole Ramsay
Production Manager: Todd Rechner
Production Coordinator: Tessa Spring

Colour reproduction by Splitting Image Colour Studio
Printed in China by Leo Paper Product. LTD

Disclaimer The use of this book and of the website www.naturalharry.com.au is at the sole risk of the reader. Its content does not replace medical advice and is not a substitution for a physician's advice for, or diagnosis of, any health issue. The reader should regularly consult a physician in relation to any health issues. The author and publisher have no responsibility in relation to any adverse effects arising from following any advice given in this book. You accept all risks and responsibility for losses, damages, costs and other consequences resulting directly or indirectly from using this book or the relating website www.naturalharry.com.au and any information or material available from them. To the maximum permitted by law, the authors exclude all liability to any person arising directly or indirectly from using this book or website's information or material available from them.